"A clear-eyed assessment of the links between property, policing, and the subjugation of Black people … Walcott's analysis of the ways in which white supremacy is baked into the legal systems of Canada and the U.S. is stimulating."

—*Publishers Weekly*

"[If] statements such as 'the problem of property is resolved through its removal' or calls to 'abolish everything' can make some people quake, when Walcott's pamphlet argues for the human ability to reconsider and rebuild societal structures, the stances come across as sensible and, better yet, doable."

—*Toronto Star*

"Walcott's vision of the abolition of property brings with it a view of the commons as it is located in Black history and Black Life. So, it sees the whole world. Urgent, far-reaching and with a profound generosity of care, the wisdom in *On Property* is absolute."

—Canisia Lubrin, *The Dyzgraphxst*

"Provocative and persuasive. Rinaldo Walcott's insightful unmasking of the historic baggage associated with private property challenges us to face up to what might be the source of our most pressing social problems."

—Cecil Foster, *They Call Me George*

"Rinaldo Walcott is one of the most renowned and dynamic articulators of the Black radical tradition. His writings are essential for anyone seeking deeper engagement with the social and political movements urgently afoot today."

Chariandy, *I've Been Meaning to Tell You*

RINALDO WALCOTT

On Property

Policing, Prisons, and the Call

for Abolition

BIBLIOASIS

Windsor, Ontario

FIRST EDITION
Third Printing, January 2024.

Library and Archives Canada Cataloguing in Publication

Title: On property / Rinaldo Walcott.
Names: Walcott, Rinaldo, 1965- author.
Description: Series statement: Field notes ; 2
Identifiers: Canadiana (print) 20210092165 | Canadiana (ebook) 20210092297
| ISBN 9781771964074
   (softcover) | ISBN 9781771964081 (ebook)
Subjects: LCSH: Property. | LCSH: Property—Social aspects. | LCSH: Right of
property. | LCSH:
   Police power.
Classification: LCC HB701 .W35 2021 | DDC 306.3/2—dc23

Edited by Daniel Wells
Copyedited by Emily Donaldson
Typeset by Vanessa Stauffer
Series designed by Ingrid Paulson

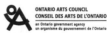

Published with the generous assistance of the Canada Council for the Arts,
which last year invested $153 million to bring the arts to Canadians throughout
the country, and the financial support of the Government of Canada. Biblioasis
also acknowledges the support of the Ontario Arts Council (OAC), an agency of
the Government of Ontario, which last year funded 1,709 individual artists
and 1,078 organizations in 204 communities across Ontario, for a total of
$52.1 million, and the contribution of the Government of Ontario through the
Ontario Book Publishing Tax Credit and Ontario Creates.

PRINTED AND BOUND IN CANADA

Contents

Set the captives free.

—Bob Marley

But I know change gonna come, oh yes it will.

—Sam Cooke

Don't you know
They're talkin' 'bout a revolution.

—Tracy Chapman

1. Property is a Problem

I WAS BORN in the Caribbean and have lived most of my life in Canada, specifically Toronto. I was always interested in politics, even when I did not have a language for that interest. I still recall, as a child in Barbados, the moment when Rastafarians began to show up in larger numbers on the island. They were immediately accused of being, and treated as if, mad. Their smoking of marijuana as a sacrament was criminalized and the religious and spiritual practices they performed were almost universally frowned upon. The Rastafarians sought to liberate themselves from their oppression in the Americas—which they renamed Babylon—by practicing a politics fully conscious of both the historical and ongoing suffering of Black people. They called this *downpression*, since there was nothing *up* about it. Rastafarians often renamed ideas to give them a more pointed, clearer meaning. The spirit of abolitionism, the first time, perhaps, I'd come across it, was encapsulated in their oft-repeated phrase "fire go bon Babylon" (fire will burn).

I realized that for Rastafarians abolition wasn't something of the past: it was an ongoing, contemporary movement, that would not be over until Black people everywhere were free, equal and safe. Rastafarianism was infused with a rebellious spirit that has shaped my worldview. Rastafarian refusal of a wide range of knowledges and their invention of new ways of being together have stayed with me as a powerful practice of self-determination. Their influence is marked on my body by my wearing of dreadlocks, but more importantly, their example of rein-vention has marked my thinking. I invoke the Rastafarians here, at the beginning of this essay, because they repre-sent for me how transformation can happen in the midst of ongoing forms of subjection and suffering. But I also invoke them because, as I have come to better understand the stakes of abolition, I believe their refusals to be one of its foundations.

One of the most important aspects of Rastafarianism, which has stayed with me all this time, is its irreverence for individual property. Rastafarians live communally, if patriarchally, and in so doing eschew property, believing it presents a significant ethical problem. Their irrever-ence has taken many different forms. What I learned from Rastafarians, even if I could not put it into words as a child, was that property was more generally a problem for Black people. Moreover, when wrapped in individual as opposed to collective ownership, property brought with it tremendous violence. I still recall too many images of young Rastafarian men being taken away by police and mental health workers, who claimed that they were either mad or criminal or both for "liberating," as they called it, fruit from trees, even abandoned trees, or for smoking cannabis. When asked how he could justify his extreme wealth and possessions, Bob Marley, the most famous Rastafarian of them all, famously retorted: "Possessions make you rich? I don't have that type of richness. My richness is life forever." Marley succinctly captured Rastafarian philosophy with these few pithy words. It is this approach to life, borrowed from the traces of Rastafarian philosophy, that has characterized my own philosophy ever since.

Growing up as I did in a post-slavery society, where one is acutely aware of one's status as the descendant of slaves, there exists a largely unspoken but palpable understanding within the Black community about property and its relationship to abolition. It was still illegal in my Barbadian childhood to take a few pieces of cane from the fields, a crop that had even then been in decline for many years. The irony of this shouldn't be lost on anyone. Sugarcane was the crop that historically led to the enslavement of Black people on that small island; it was because of the cane that it came to be their home. Indeed, in my youth, plantations still hired watchmen and even policemen (at that time they were *always* men) to make sure that those living near cane fields didn't take a few stalks for their personal enjoyment. This too has lingered with me ever since, and I reflect on it often. It has given me a better understanding of the sometimes hidden relationships and practices around property that have marked it in my mind as a serious societal problem. And it's also part of the rationale for why I have come to believe that, in the Americas but also across what we call the West, Black people will not be fully able to breathe—a word I do not use lightly—until property itself is abolished.

What is these days termed abolition politics is, I am going to suggest, the route to Black people's full breath.

When I heard about George Floyd's final plea for breath in Minneapolis, Minnesota, on May 25, 2020, it seemed at first merely one among many other deaths in recent years. But it also immediately reminded me of Eric Garner's similar plea when he died at the hands of police for selling loose cigarettes on the street in New York City on July 17, 2014. And these deaths linked up with other recent ones, of Trayvon Martin in Florida and Mike Brown in Ferguson, Missouri, and Jermaine Carby in Peel, Ontario, among so many others before and along- side them. But Floyd's death in the midst of the pandemic seemed to reignite the call for the urgent transformation of Black people's encounters with police, as well as of policing, in a manner more broadly construed. The COVID-19 pandemic had already set in motion numerous demands for change and for a reckoning with how we live in North America and much of the Western world, and the images and reports around Floyd's death seemed to increase the likelihood of yet another reckoning. That a Black man could be openly killed in the streets by state-sanctioned authority for passing a counterfeit twen- ty-dollar bill was not surprising to me. It was a sad truth. We had seen it before, but in a pandemic in which the possibility of death was heightened for all of us, it seemed to ring differently. Why that is the case I do not know. But Floyd's death also affirmed what many Black people like me already knew: that we have a different relationship to property and its meaning than white people and many other people of colour do. This, too, should not be a sur- prise to anyone. The issue of property sits at the centre of

Black people's relationship with policing both past and present, and it is central to making sense of why more and more Black people, alongside others who support our communities, called for the defunding of the police, prisons, and the entire judicial system in the wake of George Floyd's murder. An abolitionist future is not possible without the abolition of police. And it is my contention that this is not possible without the abolition of property.

In the days after George Floyd's death a battle cry was sounded, to defund and abolish the police. An abolitionist mood was in the air on streets across North America, in Canada as well as in the United States, and from there it spread to other countries and other continents. Enough that we could believe, if only for a moment, that real change might finally be possible. How did we arrive here? What does abolition mean in our time? And if we see abolition as a form of justice, how do we get there? More than any other idea arising out of contemporary Black social protest movements, including the recent Black Lives Matter movement, abolition has ignited imaginations in a manner that is essential for real change. For those of us who have long thought of abolition as an answer to what seems like intractable global problems of racial oppression and domination, especially where Black people are concerned, abolition's loud arrival in this moment, in the eventful circumstances of George Floyd's death, was thrilling to see and reason for at least a cautious optimism. Not since the fall of the Berlin Wall in 1989 have we witnessed a global cry for freedom like it.

It is important to note that many leading abolition figures, like the internationally celebrated African-American

activist Angela Davis, came to their political positions
through a radical politics of Black power and communism. Abolition has come to occupy the place that the
promise of communism once held for many of us. Indeed,
in a recent lecture, the renowned African-American crit-
ical-feminist geographer and abolitionist scholar Ruth
Wilson Gilmore described abolition as "small c communism without a party."[1] Questions surrounding property
and its ownership remain central to any politics that has
collective practices as its foundation. Abolitionist think-
ers and practitioners foresee a future in which the
problem of property is resolved through its removal. We
do not just want to abolish the police and the courts; we
want to abolish everything. We want freedom and we
know and understand, in a way that our own history has
taught us, that abolition is the only route towards it. Our
present demand for abolition has a much longer history.

Plantation Logic and Property

THE LONG-TERM HISTORY of abolition is founded in the
historic fight to abolish the Atlantic trade in African flesh
and to end plantation slavery across the Americas. The
foundation on which present-day abolition is built is the
historic struggle to bring Black people out of slavery and
into more positive and equal relationships with property,
and white people, while ensuring their freedom of movement. David Brion Davis, in *Inhuman Bondage: The Rise*

and Fall of Slavery in the New World (2006), makes the case "that the fall of New World slavery could not have occurred if there had been no abolitionist movements."[2] Indeed, one must amend Davis to acknowledge the roles played by the enslaved as well as the formerly enslaved (freed Black people and runaways) in the abolitionist movements of that time, and in the eventual end of Black enslavement in the Americas. Key to Davis's insights into the abolitionist movement is his acknowledgement that it "should help inspire some confidence in other movements for social change, for not being condemned to fully accept the world into which we are born."[3] Davis shows that all social movements born after the abolition of slavery in the Americas borrowed tactics from the latter, and that the abolitionist movement offered a template for organizing large-scale protests (letter-writing campaigns, public demonstrations, testimonials, etc.). In our current moment, abolitionist politics attempts, as the celebrated abolitionist, activist, and community organizer Mariame Kaba has argued, to help us conceive of a world without the police.[4] However, I am also going to suggest that contemporary abolitionist movements represent unfinished business from the first abolition movements and are part of a renewed effort for a transformed global polity. The idea of abolition, then, is a significant and important challenge to the world as we have come to know it, to experience it, and to how we imagine it going forward. Abolition refuses the inevitability of our present organization of human life.

The Haitian revolution offers up one of the most compelling historical examples of the refutation of human enslavement. In his *The Black Jacobins: Toussaint L'Ouver-*

ture and the San Domingo Revolution (1963/1989), the revered Caribbean intellectual C L R James powerfully describes the profound reimagining of racial subordination and conditions that the Haitian revolution, which began in 1791 and culminated in 1804, offered enslaved Africans. James argues persuasively that the enslaved wanted to be free and shows us how they effectively organized to achieve their freedom, all while demonstrating how a series of revolts culminated in the taking of the colony fully by the slaves, followed by their declaration of independence in 1804. "The slaves had revolted because they wanted to be free. But no ruling class ever admits such things," James writes, pointing to critics of the revolution who did not want to acknowledge that the slave could have an idea of freedom for which they were willing to die.[5] Taking one's freedom is a tremendous act of abolition, and while the term abolition is not often used in reference to revolution, because the latter term seems to our ears more radical, abolition is nevertheless a revolutionary idea and practice since it demands a much deeper and newer commitment to all that it seeks to replace.

Calls for the abolition of police in 2020, then, operate within a similar dynamic and logic, one in which establishment leaders like former US President Barack Obama and President-Elect Joe Biden or Toronto's Mayor John Tory refuse to believe that the people demanding abolition actually want it, or understand what they are organizing for; while for activists, abolition is a bold demand for a different kind of freedom. Our communities' commitment to abolition continues to be minimized as irrational or uninformed, while elites of all stripes continue to undermine abolitionist movements. In the moment of George Floyd's death and the accompanying call for the abolition of the police, the ruling classes, state actors and their interests, along with some intellectual elites, made the claim that those calling for abolition lacked a proper understanding of how policing works. They dismissed as emotional, irrational, and poorly thought through activists' demands to defund the police and the criminal justice system—which in this essay I refer to as the *criminal punishment system*—and to eventually abolish these institutions that orient and govern our lives.

If one reads James's account of the Haitian revolution alongside Davis's account of the abolitionist movement in the Americas, one begins to notice something else that sits as a central conundrum of abolition: the question of property. The Black enslaved were denied the legal status of family; this meant that they "passed on to their children an inherited status as being private property."[b] It was not just that one was enslaved; it was also that one could not "own" one's self and one's offspring, and therefore could not lay claim to family. In both theory and practice, this meant that the Black enslaved person literally had no autonomy or control over either their body or biological kin: the child followed the condition of the mother and thereby became at birth the white master's property. This fact has informed Black people's relationship to property ever since. Calls for and demands for abolition are built on a memory of slavery not too far removed from the present-day reality for many of us.

The problem of property and bodies, then, is at the foundation of contemporary abolitionist claims, much as

it was at the abolition movement's historic founding. In
the context of the Haitian revolution, the enslaved had to
conceive of owning themselves both physically and psy-
chically, and it is this kind of ownership that underwrites
contemporary calls for abolition. Thus, abolition as a radical politics means to create a different world, a different
set of governing relations. It is a transformation of our
society as we know it.

Having once been property ourselves, we as Black
people perhaps understand more than most the stakes of
an abolition politics and the reasons why it is necessary.
The African-American cultural critic and MacArthur fellow Fred Moten, in his critique of Karl Marx's conception
of the commodity, writes about "what Marx couldn't even
imagine, the commodity who shrieked."[7] In doing so, he
ties together Black bodies, commodities, and property
ownership, highlighting the entangled and antagonistic
web that ensnares them.[8] Moten writes about Aunt Hes-
ter's scream in Frederick Douglass's autobiographical
slave narrative, highlighting her ownership by the slave
master alongside evidence that she is an independent
sentient being or life form, and one therefore not totally
captured by the subordination, or *thingification*, of her
enslavement. It is indeed the gap between the commodi-
fied ownership of the slave and the slave's refusal of this
status, and their insistence on being more than their subordination and *thingification* allows, that gives birth to
abolition as a reimagining of what life can be. It is also
why abolition as an idea and a practice has taken root in
Black communities the world over as an alternative way
of organizing themselves and living their lives. Black
people, historically and at the present moment, have nec-

essarily become adept at resisting, silently and otherwise, the *thingification* that has been thrust upon them by others, and it is in this resistance, this refusal, that abolition's seed has taken root and grown.

Policing is central to all abolitionist claims. As a people who have been "policed" from the plantation straight through to the present moment, Black people have such an intimate understanding of what policing looks like in all its forms that imagining a world without police is only logical, often urgently so. That there was ever a world without police should not surprise anyone, though I also know it will. But there is a beginning to everything, including the police, which is another way of saying that there was a time when things could have been different. In her essay "The Long Blue Line," Jill Lepore, a columnist for *The New Yorker,* summarizes the historical emergence of policing in the Americas. Lepore makes a distinction between monarchial policing, such as what happened in pre-discovery England, and what developed in the colonies. In England, constables and watchmen kept peace for the king, thus claiming the kingdom as the king's home. Lepore explains that maintaining "the king's peace became the duty of an officer of the court called a constable, aided by his watchmen: every male adult could be called on to take a turn walking a ward at night and, if trouble came, to raise a hue and cry."[9] In the colonies, a different set of relations developed. Lepore points out that the earliest special forces, or police, were created for the express purposes of "policing" enslaved Black people in my birthplace, Barbados, Britain's first sustained colony in the Caribbean region. Lepore calls this first instance not the rule of law but the rule of the police. By the rule of police we mean that posse-like bands of white men were endowed by landowners with the power to claim the land as the landowners' home. This posse-like police force could also insist on governing all aspects of a slave's life, especially with regard to movement. The Barbados model was later exported to and adopted in colonial Virginia, and spread from there across colonial and pre-revolutionary America, meaning that most of the earliest police forces in what became the United States existed almost exclusively to police—and in this instance "terrorize" might make a suitable synonym—Black people. Every European colony in the Americas eventually adopted similar systems and laws. The initial laws established in the Virginia colony listed things slaves could not do, like arm themselves; carry a club, gun, or sword; or leave the plantation without a master's certificate. Nor could a slave legally lie, hide, or injure anyone. For each of these transgressions a recalcitrant slave could be apprehended by a constable and a range of punishments inflicted on them, up to and including death. Lepore further notes that in places like colonial New York, Black people—whether enslaved or freed—were required to carry a lantern if out after sunset and were prohibited, among other things, from gathering in groups, all of it aimed at regulating how they moved around. The ghosts of these policies, as we will see, still exist throughout North America today.

Out of these types of laws and systems emerged slave patrols, which did not merely seek to return runaway slaves but to become a significant threat and menace to freed Black people. Steve McQueen captures this menace in his film *12 Years a Slave* (2013), an adaptation of Solomon Northup's memoir recounting how he, a free Black man from New York State, became abducted into slavery. The history and template of policing, Lepore argues, which is founded on the idea that Black people are always suspect, underwrites contemporary policing in the US. It has also, I firmly believe, come to underwrite policing more generally wherever large numbers of Black people exist.

The understanding that modern policing has emerged out of the dreadful history of Black enslavement brings with it an urgent need to acknowledge what is not yet behind us. The plantation isn't, as so many of us, Black and otherwise, think or at least wish to believe, a thing of the past; rather, the plantation persists as a largely unseen superstructure shaping modern, everyday life and many of its practices, attitudes, and assumptions, even if some of these have been, over time, transformed. In her essay "Plantation Futures," Katherine McKittrick, the Black feminist geographer, argues that the plantation remains the primary model for modern ideas of service, how cities are organized, who is valued, and so much more. McKittrick believes that the plantation has not gone away but has rather been diffused, shaping innumerable aspects of modern life.[10] Indeed, the ideas forged in the plantation economy continue to shape our social relations, and those historic social relations, in turn, have consequences for how we encounter each other in the present and how we then process these encounters.

One of the most significant ideas to flow from the plantation is the logic of possession, and how it extends all the way from property to various cultural practices and who possesses the power and authority in all manner of social relations in our culture. In *They Were Her Property: White Women as Slave Owners in the American South* (2019), Stephanie E Jones-Rogers delineates the way in which Southern law worked in terms of ownership. Jones-Rogers's account of white slave-owning women alerts us to the complicated nature of slavery, and in so doing points to the important codes of management, regulation, and law-like practices that grew up around it.[11] These were used to construct a social and cultural scaffold that positioned white women, who, in a patriarchal society, were normally subservient and in a lower legal and social position to men, in positions of power and authority over Black beings, men and women alike. Because the slave was a sentient, labouring commodity, managing the slave, as well as others who interacted in various capacities with him or her, required the establishment of rules, practices, etiquette, and laws. This management also required that special status be given to white women exclusively in their relationships with enslaved and free Blacks alike.

At the same time, recognizing that the slave was a sentient being who had to be subordinated into their status also required rules, laws, and etiquette for such subjection to be maintained and for it to appear normal and natural. Possession had to be something more than ownership, so it also became authority invested in white people to direct all inferiors. This meant that even when a white person did not actually own slaves, he or she still possessed authority over Black people, whether enslaved or not. Jones-Rogers has shown us how the contract law and management systems that were created and developed to manage the rights of slave owners and non-slave owners also produced social practices whereby white people came to see themselves as having "management" and regulatory power over all Black people. This management and regulatory power evolved, in a post-slavery world, into a cultural attitude in which white people's sense of superiority and understanding of the social contract came with an expectation that Black people would practice subordination in a number of different ways. This cultural performance of Black subordination is what Toni Morrison, in another register, called "grumbles and apology," and it continues in various forms and manners in the present day.[12]

These questions of possession and subordination become central to what the African-American feminist Saidiya Hartman, another MacArthur fellow, historian, and cultural critic, has called "the afterlife of slavery." Writing about the Black Codes, or the laws that came into being after the American Civil War to manage freed Black conduct and movement, Hartman lists racial classifications, bans on interracial sexual liaisons, social association, terms of contract, and rules of appropriate conduct as the conditions that brutally managed Black life in the emancipated US.[13] Hartman maintains, and I concur, that "Like the freedmen's schoolbooks, the Black Codes and contract system mandated forms of dutiful and proper conduct. Unmistakably, the proper spirit was one of submission."[14] While Hartman is focused on the US, similar practices, expectations, and enforced brutalities existed in every post-slavery society in the Americas. The practices Hartman outlines are best seen in Canada through its segregated schools and the related actions tied to them. From about the 1840s onwards, Black Canadians were forced into all manner of segregated social life. The legal scholar Constance Backhouse used the term "colour-bar tactics" to describes these practices, which took different shape and form across the country. It wasn't until the late 1940s that statues against racial segregation in public places like hotels were put into place.[15]

There are histories and stories of places throughout the Americas, even in putatively Black countries, where Black people know not to go, even today. Now that tourism has replaced the plantation as the primary sources of revenue in many of these regions, places frequented by tourists (who are almost always assumed to be white), like certain higher-end bars and restaurants, are often off limits to Black people. These new plantations by the sea, as Derek Walcott, the Caribbean Nobel Prize-winning writer and artist, called them, are shaped by the long history of the older plantation model still.[16] In many countries beaches and parks are also off limits, if only informally, as are the neighbourhoods of the small-pocketed descendants of white plantocracy, even after all these years. The gated condominium and time-share communities that have sprung up share similar dynamics. Black people only show up in these places as (service) labour, as police and private police, or, on rare occasions, as exceptionally rich individuals whose wealth buys access normally denied. But by and large Black people retain an outsider status in such spaces.

These are places where the police will question Black people for just being present. These are places where Black *out-of-placeness* is a signal of the long and enduring history of Black subjection. And in a post-slavery world, these are places where the unspoken attitudinal practices of slavery, fully born from the plantation's womb, still fashion social relations. Black people know these places and share stories of them among themselves. Black people know the attitudes of these places too. Black people feel, deep in their bones, that these places should not exist. In short, these are places worthy of abolition. The plantation's afterlife extends to these places, and it also helps to set and manage the social relations that shapes our interactions within them.

To fully comprehend Black people's desire for abolition as a politics worth fighting for and as a philosophy orienting how we live together in the future, it is important to note all the ways in which the history of Black enslavement in the Americas continues to shape our current existence. The afterlife of slavery is in part a set of social relations between Black and white people in which it is often assumed that Black people should practice some form of subordination. Black people continue to resist forms of ownership, subordination, and possession in both conscious and unconscious ways—by ourselves and others. Black people have had to actively work to refuse and resist being reduced in this way, in order to exist in a world perceived to be made for white fulfilment only.

In writing about how the logic of the plantation and of slavery shaped the segregated US, C L R James tied lynching to forms of agency and labour control, noting that when cotton was booming lynching decreased, and that when the economy became difficult for poor white people, lynching was left unchecked. He points out that most lynchings occurred where a Black labour force wasn't needed. Indeed, even in our neoliberal times, policing is most active where the poor, the unemployed, the Black, and the disposable are segregated. Lynching was primarily a technique of control, and because it so often went unpunished, it further helped to develop conscious and unconscious attitudes about the value of Black life. But lynching also helped to solidify the idea in white communities that Black people could not be trusted, and that the only way to control them was through a severe hand. Lynching also served to put in place and secure broader social attitudes concerning how Black people should govern themselves when in the company of white authority.

The Black Canadian historian Barrington Walker, writing of Canada, notes that:

> Dating back to the mid-19th century, blacks in Canada have been unfairly treated in the criminal justice system, subject to higher rates of arrest, conviction and longer terms of imprisonment, particularly if their crimes crossed the lines of race and sex. These patterns endured over the course of the 20th century. Indeed, the opening up of Canadian immigration policy to the new black immigrants of the Caribbean in the late 1960s gave way to a host of anxieties about race, crime, and public order in Toronto from the 1970s until the mid-1990s.[17]

One can extend Walker's historical account into the present, as I will show later. The point being made is that the sensational examples of violence against Black individuals and communities in the US have lesser known and only slightly less sensational counterparts elsewhere, especially in Canada. What I am therefore diagnosing is a global Black condition and set of practices and outcomes that cross borders wherever Black people are. The history of policing and its deadly consequences for Black people is therefore not an issue bound in by national borders, and it is this understanding that has resulted in cross-national solidarities for Black people as they call for abolition in many different geopolitical contexts.

Black people, once owned as property and now the main (if not the exclusive) target of mass criminalization and incarceration and all the not-so-deadly and deadly actions of modern policing and its extensions, understand that property remains a central roadblock in our collective quest to figure out how to both live differently and better together. In the following pages I will not only be suggesting that the abolition of policing and incarceration are necessary for Black people to have their full lives and their full breaths acknowledged, I will be arguing that the abolition of property is also central to this endeavour. It is precisely because of Black peoples' intimate relationship to property as both an idea and an actual practice as a result of having been property ourselves, that we understand that the entire carceral network and the innumerable problems that afflict it are intimately bound up with modern conceptions of property, because in many ways we are the foundation of the idea itself. I am not making a case for Black people's exceptional experience as an oppressed group. History, recent and ancient, has already made this exceptionality abundantly clear. I am suggesting that our long history of *thingification*, and how we have resisted it, stands as a

political and intellectual blueprint for how we can transform all of human life. We know that some of the
ghastliest experiments in the history of the last five hundred years or more have been enacted on Black people
and we further know that to recover from those experiments something more radical than reform is
necessary.

One of plantation slavery's most important and still
living legacies is the diffusion of the ideas that came
along with it and how these ideas influence policing in
both its broadest and most restricted forms. Given that
modern policing in the Americas, as we have discussed,
was created to police the property that was Black flesh, it
should not be surprising that policing continues to
remain hostile and brutal to Blacks in the Americas; and,
one can confidently say, beyond the Americas too. Policing is central to how Black people experience life even
when they are not having encounters with the actual
police, because white people remain, as Frank Wilderson
III, a co-founder of the Afropessimism school, put it,
"deputized" all the time.[18] This is just one of the ways that
the plantation persists, shaping actions, attitudes, and
behaviours. White deputization works to police Black
people in all manner of ways, especially in the West—
from modes of speech, dress, and attitudes to suspicion,
threat and assumed danger. The archetypal figure of the
big, threatening Black man is an important element of
this dynamic, alongside the belligerent, angry Black
woman. Long embedded and cemented stereotypes of
Black people are often experienced and understood to be
threats to white people and their ideas of what is appropriate and even safe; threats that therefore must be

subdued or policed. Of course, this form of banal, every-day policing can and often does result in more official state policing too.

The recent phenomenon of the "Karen," or "Amy," the figure of the white woman (actual women, yes, but also both caricatures and memes) who calls the police on a Black person just for living his life and occupying a certain space at a certain time, offers us a spectacular example of white deputization. We can all recall the case of Amy Cooper and Christian Cooper (no relation) in Central Park in New York City, on May 25, 2020, the exact same day a Minneapolis police officer pinned George Floyd's windpipe under his knee. Christian Cooper reported that he had asked Amy Cooper to put her dog on a leash in a part of the park reserved for bird watching, a place where it was required that dogs be leashed at all times. Amy Cooper responded to this reasonable request by threatening to call the cops and reporting that an African-American man was threatening her life. Which she in fact did, calling 911. We know this because Christian Cooper recorded their interaction and later posted it online. If one searches the internet, one can find recording after recording of white people not allowing Black people to enter buildings, presumably because they assume Black people do not belong there; of white people attempting to prohibit Black people from using parks and other public spaces and amenities; and a wide range of regular white people attempting to regulate, contain, and prohibit Black people's use of public and private space. The thing is that, in most instances, these white people have not been invested with any authority to do so. They have, in effect, deputized themselves in their encounters with Black people. These recordings have become a genre of their own, whereby "Karen" or "Amy" refuse to let Black people live their lives, with all the usual assumptions about blackness and property integral to these interactions.

Or take the example of sagging pants, which involves the same problems of capital, Black bodily autonomy, and the ways in which both the state and individuals intervene in numerous ways to circumvent small acts of Black freedom, or even the assertion of its possibility. Sagging pants were popularized as a style in the 1990s by skaters and hip-hop artists, and though the style's origins aren't entirely clear, it seems to have first become a trend in the prison system, either because prisoners were often given poorly fitting clothes and no belts, or because they used it as a sign of nonconformity, or both. Later in the 90s, Black youth began wearing sagging pants as a symbol of freedom and the rejection of the values of mainstream society. Ordinances banning sagging pants were passed in cities like Ocala, Florida; Shreveport, Louisiana (later repealed); Pikeville, Tennessee; and Wildwood, New Jersey, among other places, and stand as examples of how official bodies attempt to curtail Black bodily autonomy and freedom. Black men sagging their pants may be an attempt to attain some measure of control over their bodies, but it is nevertheless a refusal of white norms of comportment and thus must be interdicted and punished. Black people are not supposed to own their bodies. When Black people like Obama speak out against sagging pants and other forms of youthful Black style, what bothers them is that it references a much deeper refusal, whereas I contend that it is part of an ethic that attempts to keep alive forms of Black resistance that animate Black life beyond capital.

Policing as a practice is not only at the nexus of Black and white antagonisms, it is central to antagonisms within and across Black communities too. The logic of policing in its modern manifestations means that even in Black countries policing operates with similar assumptions, though often crosscut with class antagonisms. As such, it produces similar brutalities. In majority Black countries in the Americas, race and class often work to produce enclaves of whiteness—in phenotype and in practice—that enable forms of policing that mark working class Black people as available to harsh policing methods and practices. In October 2020 a Nigerian movement called End SARS, calling for the end to the Special Anti-Robbery Squad (SARS), which has been accused of extra-judicial killings, theft, and abuse, gained international attention for its resistance to police brutality in what is largely a Black country. (It's perhaps worth mentioning that SARS members were largely trained by British authorities.) In Toronto, TAVIS, or the Toronto Anti-Violence Intervention Strategy, has operated in a similar fashion, focusing on what we euphemistically call priority neighborhoods, meaning mostly the poor: Black, Indigenous, people of colour, and poor white people.

What all of this strongly suggests is that policing as an institution remains rooted not only in the violence of the plantation, but in an even older violence: the violence of the logic that allowed Black people to be justifiably enslaved in the first place, which flows from the violence of ranking and valuing human lives in a radically unequal fashion. These forms of violence continue to underwrite policing, and its own violence, regardless of the community or country in which the policing is taking place; indeed, regardless of who is doing the policing. Plantation logic still frames present-day policing, and, as previously shown, the organization of many aspects of our day-to-day life. As those most familiar with its structure and consequences, Black people are in a unique position to see what others might not be able to. Whether anyone listens, is, of course, an entirely different question: the logic of white supremacy still governs and determines what counts as legitimate knowledge of the ruling order, and therefore Black peoples' abolitionist dreams are often deemed impossible. It was for these reasons, perhaps, that in the aftermath of George Floyd's murder, activists who had long worked for abolition were pleased to see how calls to defund the police came to occupy such a prominent place in the protests that engulfed North America and other places around the world.

We are supposed to believe, if we think about it at all, that modern-day policing is unmoored from its historical past and its beginnings rooted in slavery. Yet examples of historical practices giving birth to current ones are everywhere. Take, for example, what in many police jurisdictions are often called street checks, or carding in Ontario, and stop and frisk in places like New York City. Carding is part of the long history of travel passes, which date directly back to plantation and urban slavery. Even in urban historical slave-holding centres like Montreal, Halifax, and Fort York (colonial Toronto), slaves and freed Blacks, in order to freely move around, required passes to prove their status to the white people who demanded them. More generally, slaves who ventured outside of their master's homes or off their plantations could be required by any white man to prove, usually in the form of a note, that they had their master's permission to move around. This practice, later modified, was codified in racially segregated places through pass laws and in the form of passbooks, which were documents that confirmed "legitimate" travel. But it also showed up in nations likes South Africa, which segregated Black people into ethnic or tribal homelands, and in the way countries like the US, Canada, Australia, and New Zealand placed Indigenous people on reservations according to tribe. In fact, South Africa modelled its own passbook policies on what it saw in Canada, the US, New Zealand, and Australia, while its segregationist policies were modelled on American reservation systems. Scholars Pierre Bélanger and Kate Yoon point out that countries like Canada and South Africa have partaken in a kind of colonial exchange in which the "transfer of colonial knowledge globally" resulted in the adopting of similar policies and practices.[19] In 2010 the *Toronto Star* published a timeline entitled "A history of missteps," in which it was noted that in the 1940s, "Inspired by what it has read about Canada's Indian Act and its legal classification of 'status Indians' the South African government examine(d) Canada's Indian reserve system and later model(led) elements of apartheid after the Canadian system."[20]

The legacy of pass laws was evident in the unwritten rules and codes of communities such as sundown towns; that is, towns in the post-emancipation Americas where Black people knew they should not be found once darkness fell, or they would make themselves vulnerable to bodily harm. Sundown towns, and places like them, were based on the assumption long central to plantation logic that Black and other non-white people are always out of place and do not legitimately belong anywhere that large numbers of white people reside, especially in places now assumed to be white homelands. In a post-slavery world, such practices work to devalue Black citizenship, rendering it less-than-citizenship.

The history that underwrites practices like carding springs from slavery and its afterlife. And while these practices are now often recast as being about safety and security, the fact that they target the same groups of people as the earlier laws makes the truth abundantly clear to anyone who really cares to consider the matter. In a city like Toronto, 27 percent of all carding documented in 2013 involved Black people, a vastly higher proportion than their 8.9 percent share of the municipality's population. Indeed, it is the awareness that this dreadful history and its most brutal practices continues that motivates Black peoples' demands for abolition. Carding and similar practices create continuity between plantation slavery and the present moment, reminding Black people of their struggle for agency, autonomy, and, ultimately, to own their own bodies.

A central problem with policing in its modern manifestation is that it cannot escape its founding in slavery, the aftermath of that founding, and how that founding continues to shape its present practices. The outcome of policing's dreadful anti-Black legacy is that its practices seem inexorably more focused on those who were targets in its earliest days: Black people. Activist and organizer Mariame Kaba contends, and I agree, that:

There is not a single era in United States history in which the police were not a force of violence against black people. Policing in the South emerged from the slave patrols in the 1700s and 1800s that caught and returned runaway slaves. In the North, the first municipal police departments in the mid-1800s helped quash labor strikes and riots against the rich. Everywhere, they have suppressed marginalized populations to protect the status quo.

So, when you see a police officer pressing his knee into a black man's neck until he dies, that's the logical result of policing in America. When a police officer brutalizes a black person, he is doing what he sees as his job.[21]

Anyone who came of age in the 1980s and the early 1990s, as I did, will remember how indelible the war on drugs was at the time. The nightly news was filled with images of SWAT teams breaking down doors and arresting Black people, reports of robberies and other street crimes plaguing urban areas. Invariably, the accompanying image on the television screen, whether in the form of a mug shot or otherwise, was usually of a Black person. Young Black men were presented as violent and dangerous, the crack era's principal antagonists. Black women populated daytime television talk shows, like Phil Donahue's and Jerry Springer's, to repeatedly reprise their roles as crack mothers and unwed welfare queens giving birth to crack babies. The crack epidemic was so closely aligned with blackness that a forum was once organized at Harvard University entitled "The Black Intellectual in the Age of Crack."[22] The associations built during this period between Black people and crack did not just affect the families who were legitimately impacted by the drug; it cast a much larger net that affected the Black community emotionally, politically, socially, and spiritually. The government's focus on drug use and users as opposed to drug distribution led to laws and legislation that sent countless members of the Black community to prison for possession, breaking up families and causing even more poverty, misery, and addiction. Drug use became yet another way to suggest Black depravity, idleness, vagrancy, and lawlessness. It also justified the need for Black people to be specially policed. The devasting effect of policing on Black communities during the war on drugs remains a central aspect of abolitionist politics today.

The war on drugs also revealed the significant disparity between how white and Black people with the same quantity of drugs for personal use were treated. There is no need to ask who got off more lightly. The 1997 passage in the US of a crime bill focused on drug possession set the stage for a rapid increase in imprisonment, one that disproportionately affected Black communities and paved the way for what scholars call the prison industrial complex to become a significant aspect of the United States economy. The industrialization of imprisonment provided employment for many white people displaced by the de-industrialization of North American labour, while resulting in incarceration for others, many of them Black, recently made even more disposable by the loss of jobs to foreign shores and the further undermining of the social safety net by neoliberal politicians.

The continual focus on street gangs and street crime by police and in public policy discourse only serves to further spread the idea that Black people are more criminal than others. Michelle Alexander, in *The New Jim Crow*, whose title alludes to the way Jim Crow-like laws continue to shape society's relationship to Black people, writes: "The stark reality is that, for reasons largely unrelated to actual crime trends, the American penal system has emerged as a system of social control unparalleled in world history."[23] In the post-civil rights era, and more specifically in the post-Reagan era, a series of crime bills in Western multicultural and multiracial locales targeted Black and other non-white people for crimes, leading to their mass incarceration while giving birth, activists have argued, to the prison industrial complex. Many of these laws targeted drug and property-related crimes and led to the imprisonment of Black men and women in staggering numbers. Currently Black people make up only 12 percent of the United States' population but account for 33 percent of all its incarcerations.[24]

The war on drugs was followed by the war on terrorism, and through it all, state-funded police institutions of all kinds have been given more and more power, with private police playing a larger and larger role within the policing apparatus. Communities have been encouraged to think of themselves as constantly under siege from crime, with policing offered up as the only solution. Policing has been the main response to deindustrialization and the social disintegration that has arisen in its wake, and we have mostly internalized policing as a way to feel and believe that we are keeping bad things at bay. In short, policing is dependent upon faith and the enduring belief that some wrong might happen to us. The belief that policing is central to managing a society, especially one

in the throes of what Ruth Wilson Gilmore calls "organized abandonment," has become so ingrained as to seem
natural. Deindustrialization and the emergence of a neoliberal economy in which the welfare state has been
significantly undermined, meaning that we have all
become responsible for our individual selves, has been
balanced against increased investments in policing of all
sorts—from actual police to social workers to teachers
and others deputized to make sure that artificially
induced scarcity isn't abused by those most in need. Of
course, Black people in large numbers found themselves
among the dispossessed and disenfranchised and therefore over-policed and slated for incarceration.

In Canadian cities like Toronto, Montreal, Vancouver,
and Winnipeg, models of policing intended to interrupt
street crime, drugs, and other misdemeanors largely produced by and through poverty, also became the focus of
most policing from the 1970s onwards. Western crimi-
nal-law reform focusing on street and drug crimes,
accompanied by significant increases in punishment,
became the trend alongside new prison construction to
house convicts. In each of the above jurisdictions, Black
and Indigenous people found themselves targets of policing that singled them out as the most likely suspects,
especially for what is called street crime. Though community policing and the hiring of "minority" police officers
became a central tool of the reform-minded, it was implic-
itly understood that these hires would allow the police to
further penetrate the communities thought to be at the
root of these crimes. Indeed, in Toronto, where over the
years an escalation in gun crime in Black communities
has led to severe crises within them, the 2006 founding

of the Toronto Anti-Violence Intervention Strategy drew from the legacy of urban policing so forcefully inaugurated in the US with the 1997 crime bill. The pattern of urban policing focused on drugs and related crimes of poverty set by Reagan's war on drugs and Bill Clinton's crime bill has had a significant impact on Black and other non-white and poor communities in the US and wherever similar policies and practices have been adopted.

The notion of "broken window policing," put forth by criminologists, suggests that social environments are predictive of where criminal activity is most likely to occur. Coupled with various three-strike laws, it has become a foundation of the prison industrial complex. The theory behind broken window policing implies that anti-social behavior, vandalism, loitering, public drinking, jaywalking, fare evasion, and other by-products of poverty signal the potential for even more serious crimes. Since at least the mid-1990s, this form of policing has targeted poor, urban communities where Black people live, breaking families apart and grooming younger Black people to enter the system through practices like carding—often the first instance when a young person's personal information is entered into computerized systems. Later, the existence of that information will be used to claim that a youth is "known to the police."

The mass criminalization and imprisonment of Black people has been devasting for Black sociality and thus disruptive to ongoing community formation. At the same time there are those within Black communities that believe in the current carceral model: abolition remains contested terrain. It is still a very long journey towards what is yet to come.

One cannot stress strongly enough how images of Black people as social pariahs of one kind or another continue to frame much of the Western world's culture, in a way that can be drawn directly back to plantation slavery. These images, originally developed to pathologize Black people and justify their mistreatment and enslavement, have matured and deepened over the years, while being exported around the world. They serve to frame Black people as a global problem to be dealt with. Policing and other carceral practices are the tools most frequently used to deal with Black people and to reinforce our subjection. Society takes no responsibility for Black people's poverty and their social exclusion and isolation, even though the history of our continuing mistreatment and subjection at the hands of that very same society is well known; rather, our poverty and exclusion are offered as evidence of our inherent inferiority. The worst thing about this is that some members of the Black community have come to believe it about themselves, as both individuals and as a community; they have internalized ideas that were intentionally deployed to render Black people as lesser humans and citizens. It is these ideas that abolition is most concerned with destroying, and a key step in this process involves the unmaking of the carceral state.

An August 2020 poll by the new Gallup Center on Black Voices caused some controversy by suggesting that, contrary to other reports, the majority of Black Americans want the police to spend more, not less time in their neighbourhoods.[25] Only 22 percent of Black Americans, according to this poll, favour the abolition of police departments. This has been offered up by some commentators as evidence that the gap between what

Black and other Americans want is not as wide as some have claimed. But the poll's results aren't as surprising as some have suggested. Given that policing has been offered as the only means through which violence, conflict, and harm can be addressed, it stands to reason that those suffering such harm would desire a larger police presence to address those issues. What this poll and others like it don't address is how people might respond if they were offered alternatives to the police. There is enough anecdotal evidence from activist groups and networks in Chicago, Toronto, and elsewhere to suggest that, when offered community-led and accountable transformative justice practices and processes as alternatives to policing, people often change their minds about what they actually want. From Mariame Kaba and her "Prison Culture" blog to Project NIA in Chicago, both of which are influenced by INCITE! Women of Color Against Violence and Generation FIVE, these organizations have been leaders in developing strategies and resources for enabling the process and work of transformative justice as a replacement for policing and its carceral network of power. In Canada, restorative justice and the Gladue Court, to take another example, are part of the official judicial system even though they break with many of its usual practices. The Gladue Court was specifically established for Indigenous people to respect their histories and customs, and in so doing attempts to avoid their incarceration. When a sentence is given where incarceration can't be ruled out, it is issued in accordance with Gladue principles, which take into account Indigenous identity and the history of societal discrimination against Indigenous people.

There are also a range of alternatives to transformative justice. Community accountability and restorative justice, where injured and injurious parties meet to negotiate the terms and conditions of repairing harm done, are being practiced in a number of different communities. Testimonials by women who dealt with their sexual assaults through transformative justice can be found on various feminist websites.[26] Alternative practices include banishment from the community, public statements and the acknowledgement of having caused harm, various kinds of restitution, non-contact agreements between offender and victim, and a range of other agreements and remedies specifically developed to resolve issues between parties. These approaches have been used to deal with issues like sexual violence, child sexual abuse, and even murder.[27] It is of course in the interest of current institutions to have us believe that the present models of policing are the ones best suited to address the harms we might experience. But the broad politics of abolition seeks alternatives beyond policing that don't reproduce the violence that police and prisons perpetuate. Abolition as a philosophy recognizes that harm happens, but contends that addressing one harm with another offers no way forward; rather, abolition is based on the idea that mitigating further or continued harm needs to be the priority, and that awareness is central to any form of restitution or philosophical reworking of our present system.

2. Black Resistance and Conceptions of Property

SINCE BLACK PEOPLE have a special relationship to property, having once been property ourselves, that history frames our ongoing relationship to policing. I still remember the television images of Los Angeles burning in 1992 like it was yesterday. Those images, and the mayhem that ensued, are burned into my memory. And I must admit that seeing those fires gave me a certain *jouissance*. I was in Toronto watching US news reports and identifying with the defiance of those taking to the streets in a way I could feel in my body. LA was burning, and those flames were ignited because the police officers who had viciously beaten Rodney King the year before for alleged drunk driving had been acquitted of all wrongdoing. The Rodney King beating and the LAPD officers' trial for it remains one of the first and most important cases where recorded video evidence played a role in how the public responded to police misconduct; and it showed us early on how the same recorded evidence wouldn't be treated as conclusively as we believed it would be in a court of law. The trial and the video also confirmed something else important, and something that continues to be relevant: that Black and white people largely see and indeed experience policing in radically different ways. For Black people, the police are largely experienced as a foreign and occupying force inside, as well as outside, our neighborhoods; they are seen as regulators of movement and intimidators threatening potential if not outright violence. In 1994, a controversy erupted in Toronto when a Black member of the Toronto Police Services Board responsible for oversight of the police, Arnold Minors, was quoted saying that Black people see the police as an occupying army in their community. Minors was hounded off the board for merely telling the truth: we'd be in a far better position today had the board listened to him. In striking contrast to Black people, most white people believe that the police represent safety, security, and order. These two vastly different views and experiences of policing continue to shape Black and white perceptions of what policing is for and shape the divergent ways Black and white communities orient themselves to abolition as a necessary demand for freedom.

The strange pleasure I felt seeing Black people's resistance in 1992 LA was also conditioned by personal experience. In the early 1990s, walking along Toronto's Queen Street West near the corner of Portland Avenue, I was stopped by two policemen who demanded to know my name. I refused, and instead asked them why they wanted to know it. My refusal led to the situation escalating quickly, and in a rather short space of time I was surrounded by at least six other officers, making the total number eight, all of them with batons drawn. My white woman friend began shouting at me to tell them my name because "they are going to beat you up." Above her plea I heard one of the officers say that they were looking for a white man in a pair of blue shorts who had tried to abduct a child. I was wearing blue shorts. But I was most definitely not a white man. This seemed to make little difference.

One can arrive at an abolitionist position independent of such personal experience, but encounters with police as a Black person definitely shape how you think of them and approach them thereafter. If you are Black and have ever been surrounded by police threatening to beat you up, your sense that slavery and the white master or mob have never actually disappeared is vitally manifest. Modern policing practices offer a significant and constant reminder to Black people that slavery isn't that far in our past, less than two hundred years for those of us living within what was once the British Empire; and for African Americans it is much shorter, little more than a hundred and fifty years, and that's not counting all the indignities and injustices that followed Jim Crow, making the historical timeline short enough to exist within living memories. My insistence that contemporary abolition is a continuation of an unfinished abolition movement is tied to both the sensation and reality of still being trapped by slavery's ongoing practices.

By the time of the 1992 riots in LA, and then later that same year in Toronto, I was therefore already on the road to understanding the police as a significant problem of Black life. The circumstances around the Toronto riot were so like those in LA that one could begin to deduce a pattern of Black mistreatment and policing across borders from these two examples alone. The Black Action Defence Committee (BADC), a Toronto-based activist group then largely focused on police brutality and over-policing in Black communities, had called a demonstration to show solidarity with Black protestors in LA, and to protest the police shooting of a Black man, Raymond Lawrence. At the time, anger was still simmering over the fact that, earlier that year, two officers in Toronto's Peel Region has been acquitted in the 1988 shooting death of teenager Michael Wade Lawson. It remains unclear what sparked the initial riot in Toronto. The protest had begun as a peaceful march from the US Consulate on University Avenue to City Hall, where I joined it on my bicycle. After the City Hall speeches, protestors moved on to Yonge Street and began to march north. It was a mixed-raced group of young people, estimated at about one thousand, who took peacefully to Yonge Street, but the authorities deemed it an unlawful march and began to close in. Shortly thereafter the smashing of windows and looting began. It was around Yonge and Gerrard Street that a battalion of police first appeared, escalating matters, which resulted in running battles with protestors along parts of Yonge, Bloor, and Bay streets. I was part of the Yonge Street march, and though I still have no firm idea as to what exactly sparked the uprising, I do know that watching others break windows and topple statues and other structures gave my body a liberating jolt like I had never felt before.

I was a twenty-seven-year-old young man on those streets in the early '90s, and I'd ridden to the demonstration in order to get real-life experience to inform the dissertation I was then writing on Black youth culture and rap music, which had become the dominant soundtrack of North American life. Rap's rise was accompanied by increased vilification, intensified criminalization, and the demonization of young Black men as dangerous, threatening, and disposable. The police were called upon to make real the fiction of the young Black man as the most dangerous threat to Western civilization post-Berlin Wall. I don't think this is an exaggeration. In retrospect, it is obvious to me that the riot was in part a result of a very real and significant frustration with the ongoing abuse of Black people by police and the latter's regular exoneration by the government's punishment system. In the middle of the riot, however, it felt more like an attempt to break free from a suffocating chokehold constricting our lives.

In the aftermath of the Rodney King beating it was revealed that the acronym NHI, short for "No Human Involved," was a code that "public officials of the judicial system of Los Angeles routinely used ... to refer to any case involving a breach of rights of young Black males."[28] Such attitudes and practices further demonstrated how the logic of slavery continued to underwrite modern policing and its encounters with Black people.

The similarities between the Toronto and LA riots cannot be denied by anyone who cares to notice. They were motivated by the same kinds of events, the same emotions, the same tensions between the cities' respective Black communities and the police who terrorized them.

Both further cemented my opinion that policing as an institution had a very particular relationship to Black people that remained the same regardless of where one was in the world.

In some ways, the details of the two riots matter less now than the fact that both produced and enabled an understanding of policing that remains with us to this day. They helped many, both inside and outside of Black communities, understand that the police and policing were considerably different from how they'd traditionally been presented. This change in perception resulted in increased calls for police reform, in the hope that police could do their jobs better and with less racial animus towards Black people.

The desire to maintain a system of policing but reform it so that it is less biased, or better yet, not biased at all, is central to any conversation about abolition and why it has emerged as such a powerful idea and demand. Since at least the 1970s, Black people across North America and beyond have come to understand that what is called police reform almost never has any impact on how they themselves are policed. In fact, one of abolition's foundational notions is that policing as an institution cannot be reformed in any fashion that would make it amenable to Black safety, security, and, ultimately, to Black life. What I will therefore suggest in the remainder of this essay is that the abolition of slavery was just the first stop on the abolition journey of, and for, Black people.

The remaking of the post-industrial economy from the mid-1980s in Canada and as early as the 1980s in the US until the present brought with it numerous social and cultural changes and challenges. These changes also brought with them a heightened sense of individualism and an ethos of looking out for oneself. In the context of this upheaval, workers and others displaced by the reorganized economy often took to the streets to protest, and they were often met there by the police. The most prominent of these protests in the 1980s and 1990s were those against the then G8, which later became the G20.

If you have never participated in a protest where the police are basically at war with the demonstrators then you have not fully experienced the violence that policing represents. Fully decked out in their battle gear and arranged in battalion formation, the police represent, in both form and practice, a martial force arrayed against the very civilians they are supposed to protect. I have participated in two significant protests—the 1992 uprising and the 2010 G20 protests, both in Toronto—where it was made abundantly clear that the police are a violent force instead of the opposite. To experience police on horseback and in full riot gear advancing on you in unison, chanting, shouting, with batons raised, beating their shields in time, poised and ready to strike and trample you, is terrifying. And yet people continue to face potential violence by taking to the streets to protest police and other kinds of wrongdoing. When you are in a situation where police violence is imminent, you begin to understand how the deployment of a violent institution cannot by its very nature stem violence; and can in fact only lead to increased violence. In most instances where riots break out, the police riot right back, indiscriminately beating, trampling, and abusing people. In the 1992 Toronto riots the police rushed us on horseback down Bay Street and their violence is stamped on my mind. At College and

Yonge streets during the 2010 G20 protests, battalions of police similarly surrounded us, presenting themselves in a fashion that suggested a level of violence we neither expected nor deserved. It was during those protests that I not only learned what kettling was—a practice where police literally encircle protesters, prohibiting them from moving—I experienced it. In every one of these instances the police justified their use of extreme force and violence by making the claim that property had to be protected.

What is it about property that demands that we, as a society, collectively sanction this kind of violence to protect it? The role of the riot is crucial to understanding contemporary abolitionism. It should surprise no one that Black people might riot after years of building frustrations about policing in their communities. Indeed, it is alleged that some plantation masters understood the occasional rebellion as part of the cost of slavery. Plantation owners who made their peace with runaway slaves called Maroons are one instance of this. The deals they made often allowed the Maroons to keep land and settle on it in exchange for the return of other runaways. Jamaica's First Maroon War, in 1728, was a perfect example of plantation owners accepting Maroon communities as the cost of dealing in slavery on the island.[29]

The Black riot is a refusal of entrenched policing practices that has boiled over. The riot is an expression of revolt with a historical basis in slavery. In activist circles, riots have been renamed uprisings, thereby giving their actions a deeper meaning. And the difference isn't merely semantic. Riots often garner the attention of state authorities in a way that so-called peaceful protests do not. The riot, or uprising, is an important element of the quest for Black freedom.

One might even call rioting a tradition, a claim I don't make lightly, or in jest. I make it, rather, to point out how the aftermath of rioting or uprisings by Black people across the Western world often consists of a kind of reckoning for both the state and its non-Black citizens that would not have happened otherwise. Whether we are speaking of Canada, the US, the UK, or France, the "race riot" is a signal flare marking a deep-seated refusal to carry on as usual. While I sometimes use the word riot here, as opposed to uprising, I want to be clear that I do not understand the word as pejorative; rather, I see it as embodying a tradition of Black refusal and resistance, and just as importantly, as a way for Black people to reanimate and alter the worlds in which they find themselves.

Uprisings on slave plantations consisted of a wide range of practices, from burning crops and buildings to poisonings, breaking tools and other implements, to all-out rebellion and warfare. The Bussa Rebellion that took place on Easter Sunday, April 14, 1816, in Barbados, is notable for its pitting of enslaved Black people against free whites in outright warfare and the enlistment of Black people into a Red Coat militia to fight the rebelling slaves. It is reported that about seventy of the largest estates on the island took part in the revolt. The rebels lost the fight, with about fifty dying in battle and another seventy being executed.[30] In 1831, the Nat Turner Rebellion in Virginia was another example of all-out warfare by enslaved people against slavery. The Turner rebellions killed about sixty people before they were quelled by the local militia. Turner, a slave preacher who could read and write, led the revolt and remained free for a number of months after it was put down. Once captured, he was hung along with many others. Historian David Brion Davis notes that, after the Turner revolts were defeated, laws were enacted prohibiting teaching slaves to read and write, as it was feared that education contributed to their restlessness.[31]

When the modern Black riot is understood within this genealogy, contemporary Black uprisings take on a different meaning and tenor. Within plantation slavery rebellions were an important means for the enslaved to change the conditions of their enslavement. Historians have documented how plantation rebellions led to things like the partial recognition of Black slave families, slaves being given plots of land to grow their own food, days off from work, better food and accommodation, and other compromises meant to produce a settlement between the master and the enslaved. The slave rebellion was therefore a way for the slave to achieve some negotiating power in a context where freeing himself might not yet be possible. Of course, Haiti remains the primary example of a successful slave rebellion, but even those rebellions that did not end in independence and nationhood played a significant role in the inexorable movement towards emancipation.

In this regard, two things stand out as important. Many revolt leaders, especially in the British colonies, were Christian converts who had been taught to read and were thus able to use the Bible to wage a moral argument against slavery. Secondly, as Davis notes: "In the nineteenth century, British slaves [...] showed considerable wisdom and self-discipline when they focused their violence on property and took what must have been extraordinary measures to avoid killing whites. This restraint greatly aided the abolition movement in Britain, which would surely have suffered a setback if Jamaican blacks had followed the example of Haiti and had massacred hundreds of whites."[32] Though the French couldn't defeat the Haitians on the ground, the fledgling country was nevertheless severely punished for its rebellion with an international blockade. Less successful rebellions were also met with further violence, punishment, executions, and other forms of intimidation, which might continue for weeks after a revolt was quelled to deter slaves from rebelling again. It is that culture of intimidation, derived from slavery, which continues on with modern policing, thereby producing the logical outcome whereby Black people become its main targets.

The riot, then, achieves something that other forms of protest rarely do. Importantly, it also achieves its ends more rapidly and with renewed attention and commitment from authorities. The immediate result of the 1992 Toronto uprising, for example, was the appointment, by Ontario's then-governing New Democratic Party, of Stephen Lewis to produce an analysis of the riot, along with recommendations. Lewis eschewed the more usual bureaucratic report, writing his in the form of a letter to the Bob Rae-led government, and drawing on a series of previously delivered but largely ignored reports to make the case that anti-Black racism was significantly impacting the lives of Black people in the province of Ontario, and that this should be urgently addressed. The Lewis report recommended, among other things, significant police reforms around "race relations" and for the intro-

duction of employment equity legislation. It called for a
list of education reforms rooted in multicultural and
anti-racism training for school boards and schools. It
strongly recommended changes to how the qualifications
of foreign-trained professionals and tradespeople are
assessed to improve new immigrants' opportunities for
viable employment, the striking of a cabinet committee
on "race relations," and, last but not least, a set of community development plans. The Lewis report immediately
led to the implementation of youth summer employment
and job training programs, funding for agencies serving
Black people, and the creation of other mechanisms for
combatting young Black people's alienation from Ontar-
ian society. Without the preceding riot, none of these
changes, which had a tremendously positive impact on
Black and other marginalized communities, would have
occurred. The implementation of some of Lewis's key
suggestions also resulted in the flame of resistance being
turned down a notch. In a political war of position, the
attempt to narrativize the riot as anathema to a democratic society is often merely an attempt to hold on to the
status quo of the governing order and to not respond to
the often legitimate demands of rioters.

Of course, sometimes the official response is one of
continued brutality. In 2016, Black Lives Matter Toronto
camped out at Toronto Police Services headquarters on
College Street for fifteen days. The protestors had gath-
ered at City Hall to demonstrate against the police
shooting of Andrew Loku, a Sudanese immigrant who
resided in mental health assisted housing. Loku, who was
shot almost immediately after police arrived on the scene
to quell a noise dispute that had already been resolved by

a neighbour, suffered from severe PTSD and had been in obvious distress. There is little doubt that there were ways to diffuse the situation other than shooting. Protestors marched from City Hall to police headquarters, where they set up camp, demanding that the officer who shot Loku be publicly named. The protest was peaceful, but the police responded by putting out fires built to keep protestors warm, dismantling tents, and spraying protestors with a white foreign agent. The images of these actions, captured by television cameras and cell phones, clearly show how terrifying the police can be, and that so-called "de-escalation" tactics are often meant to incite more violence. The police retreated shortly after the images made the news and the occupation carried on, but something more violent could have and most likely would have occurred had there not been a significant amount of outrage from Torontonians about police behaviour.

Police tactics like carding are often geared toward entrapping Black people. Take the case of Jermaine Carby, who was shot dead by police in Peel Region on September 24, 2014. The police reported that Carby pulled a knife on them after being stopped and carded for suspected drunk driving. A toxicology report did find amphetamines, meta-amphetamines, marijuana, and anti-depressants in his system, but Carby had only a few days prior been hospitalized for mental health and depression-related illnesses. The officer responsible for Carby's death wasn't charged with any crime. Then there's the case of Ottawa's Abdirahman Abdi, who was beaten to death by a police officer in front of his neighbours. Abdi, who had mental health issues as well, had experienced some trouble on July 24, 2016, after it was alleged that he groped women at a café that morning. Abdi was apprehended by police outside the apartment building where he lived, and neighbours filmed the arresting officers using fists and batons to subdue him. He was dead forty-five minutes later. It's alleged that one of the officers used a prohibited weighted tactical glove, something akin to a mobster's brass knuckles, in the beating. The officer was charged, in a nod to the ensuing public outcry, but was later acquitted. In *The Skin We're In: A Year of Black Resistance and Power,* Desmond Cole documents this case in detail, before concluding:

> Abdirahman was engaged in conversation with a stranger when the police arrived. If we can't imagine a different outcome than the police's violence, that's on us. We have to imagine something less violent, less reactive and reckless. Daring to imagine kindness and fairness for Abdirahman is a truly revolutionary act in a country that offers no alternatives.[33]

In both examples—though there are many, many others—the victims of police violence suffered from mental health issues. Yet both met a brutal, violent end; in Abdi's case literally at the (weighted) hands of the police. There were other ways to handle these cases, other approaches and possibilities and treatments. Take a moment: try to imagine them. But our reliance on the police in situations like these precludes other, more humane approaches. In one instance, police carding resulted in the shooting of a Black man. In the other, another Black man in obvious need of a different kind of intervention was beaten to death. These examples illustrate how violence remains the reflexive response of police, especially in situations involving Black people. And they also illustrate why calls to defund the police or for abolition are finding more and more support. There must be a different, better way to handle things.

The manner in which modern policing reproduces the same targeting of Black people as the slave patrols or pat-tyrollers of the slave-holding colonies links past and present together. For Black people, contemporary polic-ing, as Arnold Minors made clear, is often experienced as war. This feeling of embattlement becomes more under-standable when one begins to explore the difference between how Black and white people interact with the police. An Ontario Human Rights Commission study found that between 2013 and 2016 Black Torontonians were twenty times more likely to be shot by a police offi-cer than a white person.[34] This fact alone justifies Black wariness when it comes to the police; yet as we've seen, and will see again, these kinds of violent interactions between Black people and the police are just the prover-bial tip of the iceberg. White people, on the other hand, tend to see the police as helpful, or providing a necessary service.

Since the 1970s, young Black men and other non-white men throughout the Western world have been ensnared in the stereotype of the mugger, and, more recently, of the knife- and gun-wielding thug. These ste-reotypes, reinforced by police dramas and network news stories, are used to justify and legitimize what would oth-erwise be considered suspect policing practices, such as the stop and search policies that interrupt the lives and freedom of movement of young Black men and others, and which often result in confrontations. When these confrontations accumulate and become too much, riots and looting occur. In Britain in particular, the race riot has often acted as a political reset for the state's management of race relations. As such, the race riot continues the work of the slave rebellions that are its root, and which occurred throughout the former British colonies. I've previously called these riots "the return of the repressed," because they signal that, though life for Black people has changed and improved in the almost two hundred years since emancipation, the underlying attitudes that allowed for slavery to exist in the first place remain, as do some of the responses to these attitudes.

A similar history, and its looming shadow, exists in France's *banlieues*, or suburban ghettoes, especially those outside of central Paris. These are neighbourhoods where North Africans, francophone African, Martiniquan, and Gaudeloupean Black and non-white people live, many in poverty. The race riot has played a pivotal role in French Black people's resistance to ongoing racism and marginalization, a case in point being the 2005 three-week Clichy-sous-Bois rebellion, in which youth of African and Arab descent rose up after two members of their community were electrocuted while hiding from police in an electrical substation. The rioting that ensued was the result of years of frustration within the Parisian Black community about police harassment, and in particular with the use of identity checks that, under French law, allowed young people to be held for questioning for up to four hours without cause. Those who took to the streets in 2005 believed these identity checks were being egregiously misused and that they almost exclusively targeted Black people. A 2020 Human Rights Watch report entitled "They Talk to Us Like We're Dogs: Abusive Police Stops in France," a follow-up to the organization's 2012 report "The Root of Humiliation: Abusive Identity Checks in France," found that police stops related to COVID-19 lockdown measures were "over double the national average [...] in Seine-Saint-Denis, the poorest area of metropolitan France, and that 17 percent of those stopped were fined, a rate almost three times the national average."[35] It's the same old story about how modern policing and its tactics target particular groups: the descendants of plantation slavery and European colonization around the world.

Riots recently broke out again in France in response to the murder of George Floyd. The reason for the riots was partly solidarity with African Americans, but also to protest the recent death of Adama Traoré, who his family alleged had been asphyxiated by police with their bodies.[36] The similarity in the fatal techniques used by police, authorities' lack of accountability for the death of a young Black man, and Black people's testimonials about police brutality collectively amount to a powerful trans-national and cultural indictment of police and their practices. They demonstrate the violent, deadly effect police can have wherever they come into contact with Black people. The evidence keeps mounting that modern policing is the "hangover" of plantation society's "drunk" policing.

By now it should be obvious that the riots that erupted after George Floyd's murder in Minnesota are just the latest installment in a long history of such uprisings. In the US, race riots have happened regularly since shortly after emancipation, and with increasing frequency throughout the twentieth and twenty-first centuries, from Harlem (1935) to Detroit (1943) to Cicero (1951) to Birmingham (1963) and back to Harlem (1964) and Philadelphia (1964) and Watts (1965) and back to Detroit (and alongside it Buffalo, Minneapolis, Newark, Cincinnati, and elsewhere, 1967) to Baltimore (1968) and Miami (1980) and Los Angeles (1992) and Cincinnati again (2001) and Toledo (2005) and Oakland (2009) and Ferguson (2014) and Baltimore (2015), before reaching Minneapolis once more, and if history is indeed doomed to repeat itself not for the last time, in 2020. It is sad to acknowledge these riots as simply the most obvious waystations on the long revolutionary road. Sadder still to acknowledge that more still will almost certainly be needed. But this list still serves to help make clear that the riots we witnessed and participated in in 2020 are part of a continuing tradition of uprisings meant to bring the country to attention. The hope is that it might both notice and address Black suffering.

What was and remains startling about the Minneapolis riots was the burning of the city's 3rd Precinct police station. The attack on the building was deliberate and represents part of a growing movement to single out policing and its symbols. But the burning of the police station was also akin to the enslaved burning crops and buildings during slavery: it was an act meant to send a message about one of the sources of Black suffering.

In a 1967 speech at Stanford University, Martin Luther King Jr. argued that "in the final analysis, a riot is the language of the unheard."[37] This bears repeating: rioting is the language of the unheard. That this defence of rioting was offered by one of the twentieth century's leading proponents of peaceful protest should tell us all we need to know. Rioting is never just mere lawlessness. Though it is true that King's comments were immediately followed by both a condemnation of rioting as a method and an insistence on the importance of non-violent protest, in keeping with his own philosophy, these later statements do not negate the truth of his insights, which make clear King's awareness of the role rioting played in the tradition of Black uprising from the plantation onwards.

In contemporary Black rebellions looting is often a component of the uprising just like breaking tools and damaging buildings was during slavery. The purpose of looting is not stealing, at least stealing as it is commonly understood. Neither is looting about reparations, as some activists have recently claimed. Looting is a significant aspect of Black rebellion, and, consciously or otherwise, a part of a Black legacy of resistance to subjugation. In every case of significant rioting and uprising, states respond with policing and carceral action. Paradoxically carceral action is often one of the unspoken generators of uprisings because the presence of policing brings along with it the jail, the prison, and all the other mechanisms of the criminal punishment system. The carceral system therefore becomes a central site for Black protest and activism, as Black people resist being subjugated and as an outcome of said resistance, meaning that as we resist policing we become subject to policing and potentially prison too.

3. Abolition Now: From Prisons to Property

WHENEVER I DID something wrong as a small child growing up in Barbados, I was threatened with being taken to Glendairy. HM Glendairy Prison was the only institution of its kind on the island and it was both scary and a touch mythical, too: no one knew anyone who had ever actually served time there, but we'd all heard whispers about people who knew people who had. Sadly, not knowing someone in prison or someone who has had recent interactions with the police is a luxury Black people now only infrequently have.

Glendairy Prison was built in 1855 and decommissioned in 2005, after being replaced with HMP Dodds. Glendairy remains a word that always portends for me the unspeakable. Built approximately three decades after the emancipation of slaves in the British colonies, Barbados having been Britain's first in the Americas,

Glendairy loomed as large for me as it did for all Barbadians, I now realize, because it was and continues to be a potent symbol of the still lingering effects of plantation slavery. For Black people, prisons are never far removed from the plantation and its actual and symbolic powers of control, entrapment, and the many punishments that can accrue from simply being a Black person in a society hostile to them.

Prisons remain terrifying places for most Black people; for most people, I expect. But the prison dominates our lives as Black people even when we think it has nothing to do with us. Politicians regularly point to it as a symbol of security, if a false one. The logic of law and order has so infiltrated and organized our lives as to make it one of the primary means through which contemporary social relations are routed and rooted. I mean by this that our political discourse often vacillates between economics, taxes, and security, with the latter often presented as the means through which we can maintain both our individual and collective economic advantage. As such, it has come to shape our social relations.

In 2003, the African-American intellectual, international activist, and renowned prison abolitionist Angela Davis posed an urgent question, one we all need to consider, with the title of her essential book: "Are prisons obsolete?" After George Floyd's death and the ensuing protests, Davis was interviewed by key media about the history of and grounds for the recent call to "defund the police." When she appeared on the *Democracy Now!* news program on July 3, 2020, Davis explained:

The call to defund the police is, I think, an abolitionist demand, but it reflects only one aspect of
the process represented by the demand. Defunding
the police is not simply withdrawing funding for
law enforcement and doing nothing else ... It's
about shifting public funds to new services and new
institutions—mental health counsellors, who can
respond to people in crisis without arms. It's about
shifting funding to education, to housing, to recre-
ation. All of these things help to create security and
safety. It's about learning that safety, safeguarded by
violence, is not really safety.[38]

True abolition involves *at least* three necessary compo-
nents: defunding of the police, the disarming of the
police, and the abolition of policing as an institution. Of
course, at the same time, and indeed well before the
police are entirely abolished, we must work together to
come up with new ways to respond to conflict, harms,
and other behaviours that society collectively deems det-
rimental to living well together. It is for this reason that
the abolition of policing and the entire criminal punishment system is often perceived as utopian, a fantasy. How
can we deal with harm, whether it be to persons or property, whether it be through physical violence or other
forms of injustice, without the police? I understand that
this is difficult for many people to conceive. We have
been told so often and for so long that there is a certain
way of doing things, a certain way to get things done, to
protect ourselves and our loved ones (and our property),
that it is difficult even to imagine a different way. Which
is why imagination is so central to the abolitionist proj-

ect: the first foundational step to embracing a newfound freedom is embracing the freedom to imagine it.

For abolitionists, the increasing clamour and frequency of demands to defund the police across North America over the last few years mark a pivotal moment. The moment is one where abolition moved from utopian dreams and into actual policy and political discourse. At this moment in history, when the fascist impulses of Trumpism are one of the primary ways through which Black people experience the world, and not just Black people in the United States, highlighting how policing works as endowed state power is essential if we are to make sense of how the entire criminal punishment system works to oppress certain populations within a society, by keeping them in a proscribed place. Policing is many people's first encounter with the state and the myriad ways it seeks to control all elements of our lives. Abolition is not just about ending current systems; it is also an engaged and creative approach to social organization meant to fully transform how we live together. It is important to understand that abolition is about much more than just policing: its focus is, rather, on the criminal punishment system as a whole.

In the midst of the George Floyd protests and calls to defund the police, Mariame Kaba wrote in the *New York Times*:

> I've been advocating the abolition of the police for years. Regardless of your view on police power— whether you want to get rid of the police or simply to make them less violent—here's an immediate demand we can all make: Cut the number of police

in half and cut their budget in half. Fewer police officers equals fewer opportunities for them to brutalize and kill people. The idea is gaining traction in Minneapolis, Dallas, Los Angeles and other cities.[39]

Kaba is writing out of concern for how policing shapes American society, but her concerns cross any border where Black people live. Like Davis, she makes clear that defunding is only the first step, the goal being to abolish police. Calls to abolish the police didn't arise solely from police mistreatment of Black people and others, but from deep concern about the resource sinkhole that is modern policing.

In Toronto, the police budget accounts for $1.2 billion, or nearly 10 percent, of the city's total annual municipal budget of $13 billion. In contrast, the city's combined budget for social assistance, including employment services, financial assistance, and social supports, account for another 10 percent. Policing is the largest single publicly funded item in the city's budget, and the amount continues to grow year over year. In 2019, New York City's police budget was $6 billion, while the budget for the entirety of that city's social services was only an estimated $10.2 billion. Across nations and various jurisdictions within nations, policing is funded in radically different ways, so it is difficult to compare monies spent. However, after George Floyd's murder, the Council on Foreign Relations, a us-based think tank, produced a comparative graphic on the cost of police in democracies that further illuminates the issue. At the top of the list for international spending on police was Hungary, at 1.25 percent of GDP; the US, UK, and France were close behind, all hovering around 1 percent.[40] Canada did not show up on the list, but in 2011-2012, the last years for which I could find stats, Canada spent about 1.1 percent of GDP, or about $20.3 billion, on its criminal punishment system, so it would seem to rank high among the worst offenders. In contrast, Canada only spent $12 billion on Aboriginal Affairs and Northern Development Canada.[41] When it came to the killing of civilians by the police Canada ran second in the Council of Foreign Relations statistics, behind only the US.[42] In a CBC analysis of seventeen years (2000-2017) of fatal encounters with police called "Deadly Force," it was discovered that even though Black people made up only 3.5 percent of Canada's population, they accounted for 37 percent of police killings. The study also looked at Winnipeg and RCMP-policed rural areas and found that, in the city, Indigenous people accounted for 10.6 percent of the population but more than 66 percent of deaths at the hands of the police, while in rural areas of approximately eight million people, Indigenous people accounted for 118 deaths.[43] In a CBC analysis of 2020 data they found it to be the deadliest year in the last four years. Between January 1 and November 30, 55 people were shot by police in Canada and 34 of them died. "The majority of people shot by police were young men. When race could be identified, 48 per cent of people shot were Indigenous and 19 per cent were Black." Equally devastating was the fact that "of the nine shootings that started as wellness checks, all were fatal and four were people of colour."[44] If these kinds of statistics do not cause the reader to at the very least pause, then I fear that we have silently become a police state and such a claim is no exaggeration.

Think, for a minute, about the amount of money being spent on policing in Canada (or the United States, or wherever it is you're reading this) and about what could be achieved if that money were redirected to other programs and areas. To providing affordable housing or helping addicts? To supporting citizens suffering mental illness? To special education programs and training for disadvantaged youth? For retraining those whose jobs become redundant as the economy shifts? For more programs for new immigrants to allow them to more quickly become productive members of society? For Indigenous communities, to better serve and protect their people? Should we not at least spend as much on Crown-Indigenous Relations and Northern Affairs and on Indigenous Services as we do on criminal punishment? Abolitionists argue that budget numbers tell a story of priorities: you can follow the money to see what politicians and the societies they represent consider important. What do our own numbers say about our priorities?

One thing they do explain, abundantly, is why it is so difficult for so many to conceive of a world without police. Policing—and it should be obvious by now that when I refer to policing I am referring to the entire carceral apparatus, including prisons—is so deeply embedded in our social and economic way of life that it seems inescapable. But if we understand how it has evolved and continues to evolve and recognize how anti-Black ideas and attitudes have been central to that evolution, we can begin to understand why reprioritizing the resources allotted to policing is essential if we are ever to move beyond the barest of surface reforms. The percentage of our national GDP that we spend on policing needs to be understood as a choice about how to organize our economy. But we can make better, different choices. And if we understand modern policing as a part of an economy, we can begin to conceive of transforming it, as we do with other aspects of our economy, including transforming it out of existence. When we can begin to imagine a future in which policing is no longer an option in the labour market, we will begin to be able to make different local and national economic choices. It is only then that we can begin to redress policing's historic damage, which underwrites the violent founding of the American nation states; a foundation that includes transatlantic slavery as well as plantation and urban slavery and their afterlives. It is only then that the abolition movement, a movement that began centuries ago, will finally have achieved its stated purpose.

Policing often represents our first encounter with a larger ecosystem of punishment. As such, it is meant to give the impression that punishment will be dealt to those who transgress. Police are part of the necessary theatre of security, important if only to help us achieve a banal sense of safety, by which I mean one that we don't need to think about every day. At least some of us; others, however, like myself, must think about the police often. Policing is for most of us therefore often experienced as part of the "natural order" of things. Its omnipresence shapes how we understand order. It is the singular lens through which we view violence and conflict. It is understood by many to be the means through which certain kinds of harm and transgression are significantly reduced in our lives. Police therefore exist, even if most of us will never need to interact with them in our lifetimes, as one of the main ways we supposedly prevent society from descending into barbarism. Policing's ultimate force and legitimacy, then, lies in its ability to make us feel secure in our everyday lives as we internalize the belief that it functions to prevent our endangerment. As activists continually point out, policing and its best qualities exist primarily in our minds. But when we examine how it actually works in our lives a different story emerges. Activists have already shown us the ways that conflicts like sexual assault, violent crime, robbery, and even murder, for which we have come to believe we need the police, can be dealt with in order to eliminate the pervasiveness of policing in our lives. In short, there are other ways to deal with and resolve such conflicts.

The surprise expressed after George Floyd's murder about how widespread and vocal the calls were to defund the police was in part surprise at how many people had come around to the idea of defunding and abolition since 2014, when the Movement for Black Lives re-emerged after the acquittal of George Zimmerman for the murder of Trayvon Martin. Activists and activist-scholars working for prison abolition were happy to witness the fraying of the ideological claim that policing made us safe or safer, as it gave way to the understanding that police are in fact a fundamental contributor to the violence in our society. Therefore it is politically satisfying to witness as more and more people come to realize that policing itself is a form of violence rather than an end to violence. People from different communities and backgrounds are increas-

ingly educating themselves about the inequalities and
injustices built into what we have so carelessly come to
call the justice system, but which I refer to as the *punishment system*, and the central role that the police play in
creating and sustaining these inequalities.

In *Are Prisons Obsolete?* Angela Davis perfectly frames
the urgency of the abolitionist call when she writes:

> The question of whether the prison has become an
> obsolete institution has become especially urgent
> in light of the fact that more than two million
> people (out of a world total of nine million) now
> inhabit U.S. prisons, jails, youth facilities, and
> immigration detention centers.[45]

Davis then wonders if we are willing to continue to com-
mit even more people to the violence, disease, isolation,
and other maladies that come with imprisonment. The
question she poses, then, is meant to activate our imaginations to think about how we might otherwise respond
to the problems of social life without resorting to the
prison as a form of corrective discipline. "On the whole,"
Davis writes elsewhere in the same book:

> ... people tend to take prisons for granted. It is dif-
> ficult to imagine life without them. At the same
> time, there is a reluctance to face the realities hid-
> den within them, a fear of thinking about what
> happens in them. Thus, the prison is present in our
> lives and, at the same time, absent from our lives.
> To think about this simultaneous presence and
> absence is to begin to acknowledge the part played

by ideology in shaping the way we interact with our
social surroundings.[46]

No one wants to go to prison, and even those who have
experienced it try to think of it as something discon-
nected from their real, lived lives. What Davis outlines
above is not dissimilar from how policing works as well.
These two deeply interconnected and dependent institutions shape social relations, conditions, and outcomes in
ways so indelible that we would prefer not to contem-
plate the enormous function they play in our everyday
lives. It is only when we begin to become aware of the
role an institution plays in our economic life that we can
approach its transformation and eventual abolition in a
reasonable manner. Policing and its financial costs are
central to our economic organization, which means that
any significant reform or abolition of it would have ripple
effects across the economy and society.

Economic concerns are and have always been central
to the purpose and function of both the police and prison
systems. In *Golden Gulag*, Ruth Wilson Gilmore studies
the role that the California prison system plays in that
state's political economy. In what she calls "the prison
fix," she outlines how reforms to punishment and sen-
tencing, along with capital for the construction of new
prisons and the politics behind choosing the sites for new
prisons, resulted in more prisoners and in industrializing
prisoners, and how together these elements transformed
California into a carceral state entirely out of line with its
size and history. Gilmore points out that, between 1982
and 2000, the prison population in California grew by
500 percent even though crime peaked and began to

decline in 1980. She further notes that this prison population was two-thirds African American and Latino, 7
percent female, and 25 percent non-citizens. "In short,"
she concludes, "as a class, convicts are deindustrialized
cities' working or workless poor."[47] Gilmore plots how this
transformation developed from the 1970s through the
mid-1990s in observations that remain relevant to the
present day, and are equally applicable across the United
States, Canada, and elsewhere in the Western "developed" world. Of course, California's history of mass
incarceration also makes it an important place to look to
for prison reform as well.

But before we get to the question of prison reform it
remains important to note that Gilmore is intent on helping us understand the interlocking role that prisons play
in economic and state policy, and how large a role prisons
play in producing unequal wealth distribution. Deindustrialization from the 1970s onwards produced surplus
populations as well as a new labour market for workers
in prisons. In a world already riven by racial hierarchies,
white working-class labour was in many cases repurposed
for the prison industry, where Black and brown people
were the prisoners. The Federal Bureau of Prisons in the
US reports in 2020 that 62 percent of its staff are white.[48]
To put this in even more stark terms, Prison Policy Initiative, a criminal-justice-oriented American public policy
think tank, reported in 2015—using 2005 data which was
the last to which they had access—that at Attica Correctional Facility in New York State, 89.2 percent of staff
were white, while 54.4 percent and 22.6 percent of
inmates were Black and Latino, respectively, a pattern
replicated across the state.[49] And these stats are borne out

elsewhere in the US and in Canada. The prison isn't merely a place to which transgressors are dispatched for causing harm; the prison is also a central node of economic activity, from construction to courthouse to the jailing of prisoners. Consider its abolition in the light of how we make transformations in any economy. Gilmore's focus on California as "the biggest prison-building project in the history of the world" is primarily concerned with the economy and is a study of the history of racism and its transformation.[50] But more positively it is also a study of how people have organized, resisted, and found in each other the strength and organizing skills to both respond and to build the foundation for different futures through collective action.

The articulation of abolition as a central pillar of the Movement for Black Lives and its increasing acceptance at all levels of society continues Black peoples' movement towards the unfinished business of the first abolition movement that ended enslavement. The end of the slave trade and slavery was not the end of abolitionist desire or calls for social transformation. For Black people, the prison industrial complex is more than just a place, a building, a site—it is also all the other means through which Black people are confined. Parole, bail conditions, tracking and coercion technologies—these are what we have come to call the carceral state, whose tentacles involve police, prisons, lawyers, probation officers, social workers, correctional officers, and many others, including those of us, like teachers, whose employment may not even be tied directly to it. Since 9/11 the carceral state has used the threat of terror to expand its powers and to draft and deputize all of us as watchers responsible for detecting potential harm in public spaces.

The prison is the depository of all our fears. Therefore, the prison is central to abolitionist politics. But the prison is not the totality of abolition politics. Angela Davis wasn't the only thinker pressed into service to explain abolition in the days following George Floyd's death; so too was Ruth Wilson Gilmore. These scholar-activists have long worked in anti-prison and anti-violence movements, especially violence against women, and other activist configurations to transform post-civil-rights racial inequality. In a May 2020 interview with *Democracy Now!* Gilmore defined abolition this way:

> Abolition seeks to undo the way of thinking and doing things that sees prison and punishment as solutions for all kinds of social, economic, political, behavioral and interpersonal problems. Abolition, though, is not simply decarceration, put everybody out on the street. It is reorganizing how we live our lives together in the world. And this is something that people are doing in a variety of ways through-out the United States and around the planet already. It is not a pie-in-the-sky dream. It is actually some-thing that is practical and achievable in the city of New York, in Texas, in South Africa, around the world.

Gilmore wants us to understand that the carceral state is a made thing, which means that it can be unmade. What she is trying to make clear is that abolition is about choices—social, economic, and cultural—and that it places the sanctity of human life at the centre of how we care for each other. Gilmore is committed to a politics of transformation. When I have insisted at various points throughout this essay that economies are rearranged for different purposes all the time, it is because we need to get past any mental blocks people have about this fact, blocks that lead them to presume that decarceration, and eventually abolition, are impossible.

According to the John Howard Society, Canada's prison population ratio of 114 for every 100,000 inhabitants is among the highest in the developed world. Norway's prison population, for example, is only 49 per every 100,00 people, less than half of ours.[51] But the Norwegians also spend much more on education and social programs than we do. It's a question of priorities. The Canadian federal government spends about $2.4 billion annually on managing the federal prison system. Over the last five years it has increased spending by more than 20 percent, even though crime has steadily fallen. The John Howard Society also reports that provincial spending has increased even more, to $2.45 billion, up nearly 50 percent over the same period, which "is especially chilling because the largest share of the provincial costs are to keep in jail people who have not been convicted." If we take the case of Norway again, the latter spends the majority of its prison budget on prisoner rehabilitation programs, at an annual cost ranging from us$90,000 to $128,000 per prisoner.[52] At the federal level, Correctional Services Canada employs about 17,000 staff, including 7,000 guards and 4,000 administrative workers, all to manage and oversee the approximately 14,000 people currently in federal custody and 9,000 on parole.

Another 40,000 people are in provincial and territorial prisons.[53] For a population of 36 million, these are staggering numbers, and they are not borne equally by all communities: some populations, especially Black and Indigenous ones, have witnessed large increases in their rates of imprisonment.[54]

Between 2004 and 2016, the Black population in Canada's federal prisons has grown by about 70 percent and currently constitutes about 8 percent of the incarcerated population, up from 6 percent in 2002-2003.[55] This is vastly disproportionate to the 3.5 percent of the general population made up by Black people. In contrast, 72.9 percent of Canadians identify as white, but the latter only make up 54.2 percent of the prison population. In 2020, Bill Blair, the federal minister responsible for corrections, announced that, due to this apparent overrepresentation, the federal government would begin collecting specific data on the Black inmate population.[56]

But it is Canada's Indigenous communities which have suffered the most egregious treatment and fates eerily similar to those of Black people in the United States. Though Indigenous-identifying people in Canada make up only 4.9 percent of the population, they make up more than 30 percent of the prison population, or a rate six to seven times what should be expected. And as we all know, this is only one of the numerous crises affecting Indigenous people that need immediate redress. Canada's treatment of its First Nations should be a source of great national shame. An abolitionist system would ensure that Indigenous people were given the autonomy and resources to return their various communities to a healthy place.

These numbers are neither surprising nor fully capture the magnitude of the situation. Indeed, Gilmore's work on California tells us that, since the 1980s:

> The state initiated new rounds of criminalization as elected officials scrambled to sponsor new laws. The rationale for the laws purported to be reducing violence in communities. The means was sentence enhancement, or intensified "incapacitation"—to prevent people from committing crimes by keeping them in cages.[57]

The Black revolts of the mid-1960s in the US and UK, and to a much lesser degree here in Canada (it is important to understand that similar revolts happened here too, the 1969 Sir George Williams affair being one prominent example), ushered in what politicians call "criminal justice reform": an expanding of categories, lengths of incarceration, and other measures meant to make the prison a permanent element in how society manages targeted populations, while further embedding prisons in the economy. In many cases, these reforms enhanced punishments for crimes largely associated with poverty. This left Black people more at risk, due to our historic poverty, from slavery to the present. The kinds of crime that fuel incarceration cannot be divorced from the dreadful outcomes for Black lives that flow from slavery and its afterlife. Treating drug crimes, loitering, traffic and transit violations, shoplifting, and other crimes of a similar nature as significant, punishable transgressions only further exacerbates historic wrongs. And when uprisings occur in Black communities as a result of police brutality, they ironically tend to result in still more Black people having encounters with the criminal punishment system. It isn't participating in uprisings that lands most Black people in prison, but rather the business of every-day policing. The "economy of stereotype" is what leads police to stop, question, and then find some infraction, and it is far too often the way Black people get caught up in the criminal punishment system.

In 2008 my partner and I moved to a Toronto neigh-bourhood on the cusp of gentrification. The neighbourhood was known around the city as one where paid sex and drugs could be fairly easily accessed. We'd often walk north up Lansdowne Street from Bloor to Dupont, where we lived. Across from our building was a Coffee Time restaurant where small-time drug dealers and people with a range of mental health and other issues would hang out. It didn't matter what time it was: day or night, police cruisers would slow down to watch us as we minded our own business on our way home. We were never stopped, but it happened so often that we always expected we would be. I think the obvious intimacy between me and my partner, our obvious gayness, saved us from fitting too closely the stereotypes that lead to so many Black people being carded. For years, I've watched from our balcony as police officers stopped young and old alike and patted them down, searched their bags and questioned them before, most often, sending them on their way. In summer, groups of police officers would ride through the neighbourhood, stopping people head-ing home with their groceries and searching their bags, making sure no illegal drinking was happening in the Coffee Time parking lot. These were the days of TAVIS.

When I lived on the outskirts of Toronto's gay village in the late 1990s and early 2000s, I would be stopped while walking home late at night from the bars and asked where I was coming from, where I was going, did I have any drugs on me, would drugs be found on me if I was searched, what was my name, where did I live and what kind of work did I do. The white men all around me went about their business and were never stopped. Being able to say that I was a university professor and showing iden-tification to support this brought these interrogations to a quick end. I count myself lucky to have been insulated from the worst of these carding experiences. Others have not been so lucky.

Crime tends to find Black people; or, to put it another way, the police find Black people and in doing so find crime. Black people are always out of place, always sus-pect, always potentially up to no good. It is the job of police to be on the lookout for trouble, and because of the ideas and stereotypes many police have about Black people, we tend to be the trouble they are looking for. I am not suggesting that Black people don't transgress or break the law; I am rather pointing out a deeper problem. Black transgression is assumed and sought out and expected. What constitutes crime, and how criminality is assessed by those "trained" to find it, is most often cen-tered on Black people. These assumptions lead Black people to have encounters with police that lead to further entanglements with the carceral system. Sometimes those encounters result in death at the hands of the police, and Black communities respond with protests, resulting in further entanglements. It's an impossible grim-go-round, and abolition is increasingly understood by many in the Black community as the only way we can ever get off of it.

Rethinking what constitutes crime is essential and central to abolitionist philosophy. What do we mean by crime? And furthermore, why do we think that policing and prisons are the best way to deal with it? Crime in modern societies is almost entirely defined by the state, so what counts as illegal, what counts as transgression, and what counts as harm is state ordained, managed, and articulated through regulations and legislation. The state's governance of crime frees communities from having to adjudicate transgressions and descend into barbarism because the police functions as a lever between our best selves and our worst possible selves. For the police to function as the lever against barbarism we have to believe that people are naturally bad and cannot help themselves. Abolition is much less cynical, taking as a first principle that most people are essentially good; and further, that they want to be good; the fear of barbarism, based on a cynical view of human nature, is exploited by modern policing and prisons to prevent us from seeking other ways of dealing with conflict. The idea or concept of crime is ideologically deployed to stall us from figuring out how to live differently together.

Canada's legalization of cannabis in 2018 offers a case in point. The movement to legalize cannabis was not an abolitionist issue in the sense I have been discussing here, but it nevertheless points to all the problems with the carceral system. Prior to legalization, many Black people were caught up in the criminal punishment system after being charged for possession of cannabis for personal use. In 2017, the *Toronto Star* analyzed the previous ten years of data on arrests for simple marijuana possession and found that Black people with no criminal record were three times as likely to be arrested for possessing small amounts of marijuana than white people. Legalization brought little or no relief. In fact, many with possession convictions after legalization were excluded from this new industry because a key requirement of cannabis legislation was that participants not have any criminal convictions. A movement to have cannabis convictions wiped from the records of those who had been charged with simple possession for personal use failed. This has affected Black people more than many others. Why? Not because Black people are more prone to drug use, as the stereotype suggests. But because Black people, as a result of carding and other practices, are much more likely to have been stopped more than other members of the community: the law has been enforced much more severely for Black people. And when Black people are stopped the process that could lead to a longer engagement with the punishment system begins to unfold. The John Howard Society points out that "an analysis of 10,000 arrests in Toronto showed that Blacks were 50 percent more likely to be taken to a police station for processing after arrest, and 100 percent more likely to be held overnight than were whites, even taking into account criminal history and age. When given bail, they also had more conditions imposed."[58]

What we see, in the example above and elsewhere, is that there exists a certain obstinacy, a lack of grace and understanding on the part of the wider society that results in a refusal to offer any leniency to Black people who become involved in the punishment system.

What is often called police and prison reform does not and has never worked for Black people. Measures to stem police violence and other acts of harm toward Black people, like hiring more Black police officers, community policing, modernized surveillance techniques, placing police outposts in under-serviced and marginalized neighbourhoods, and starting sports camps run by police, among other programs, fail by their very nature because each is meant to further cement the position policing occupies in our lives. None of these reforms work because they do not replace the foundational imperative of modern policing: the management of Black people. Our collective refusal to contend with the truth of policing, both as an institution and a practice, means that we are willing to abandon Black people to the vagaries of a system that sees them as the very bane of its existence.

Both Mariame Kaba and Angela Davis direct us to what is possible after prisons, and, importantly, what must be achieved in the process of abolishing prisons. Again, the question of economy and collective care sits at the centre of all worthwhile alternatives. By this I mean that resources now invested in caging people must be redirected to enhancing education, health care, employment opportunities, housing and social services, among other priorities. These are the very same elements that, in the neoliberal era of welfare state reduction, have been downloaded onto families and individuals. Once we as a society come to terms with the disruptive effects of policing, we can begin to redirect resources differently, in ways that will help shape our future lives: it's only through such redirection that we can begin to create a society where prisons are no longer needed.

A world without prisons does not of course make all harm disappear, but abolitionists firmly believe that, once the basic necessities of life are secured, crimes and other social ills will eventually decrease. In places like Sweden and Norway, where prison populations have been steadily declining for years, crime has not disappeared. But prisons in these countries aren't used to deal with drug-related issues, petty crimes, loitering, and a range of other offenses that in North America serve as the main conduits through which people enter the prison industrial complex as offenders. Prison abolitionists like Kaba have long been advocates of transformative justice practices, running workshops, training programs, and acting as community liaisons to work towards achieving very specific conflict resolutions. They are preparing us for a future that they are in many ways already living through their activism, microcommunities, and philosophies of life.

During my youth in 1980s Toronto, one hardly ever saw homeless people. Only rarely did you see a person who was visibly living with mental health issues on the street. The proliferation of unhoused people and people living with mental health issues on our streets over the past twenty-five years is shocking. Or it would be shocking if we, both the housed and unhoused, hadn't become so inured to it. Homelessness has become part of the "normal" landscape of urban life. And many of us are able to identify particular people in our neighbourhoods or near our homes for whom we might have even developed some affection. There was an older Black man who used to be at the corner of St. George and Bloor streets that I had that kind of relationship with. He called me Ras, and

I called him the same. We both had dreadlocks. In such instances, we show our affection by giving money, food, coffee, sometimes even clothing, and we notice and miss these people when they disappear, as Ras did a number of years ago. I did not know his name or anything about him, really, but he was a fixture in my work life for at least a decade.

People like Ras have been abandoned by our larger society. When they most need support, that support is nowhere to be found. Yet rather than directing more resources towards services aimed at improving the welfare of these largely abandoned members of our society, we have directed more and more resources to the police. We have become overwhelmed by a vague and nameless fear of the other, the sick, the mad, of the poor and unhoused; of young, unkempt men and women rattling Starbucks cups, and we have come to believe that policing is the necessary barrier between us and those who have been abandoned. Between us and those we have abandoned.

This brings us to crux of the matter, and the problem of property. At the heart of Black people's calls for abolition is the desire to bring to a close the racial terror that we are subjected to and have been subjected to on a continuous basis since Columbus's initial voyages to the Americas. It is out of those epochal crossings, which led to the colonization of the Americas and to the large-scale, forced movement of Africans to its colonies, that many of our current attitudes, prejudices, ideas, and practices of property, contract law, insurance, banking, government, city planning, travel, customer service; indeed, all the networked elements of modern society arose. Foundational to all of it is property—private and public. It is property and our liberation from it that sets abolition apart as a philosophy capable of transforming our understanding of how to live differently together and how to reimagine what life and living can and should mean for all humans. Abolition as both an idea and a practice, then, is as epochal for the future as Columbus's voyages were for our collective past.

As I suggested at the beginning of this essay, a broader abolitionist politics is influenced by the history of communism; put in Gilmore's terms, it is a small-c communism without a party. The abolition of property undergirds a Black understanding and reworking of what communism is and means, but it is also part of a philosophy that takes the idea of the commons, meaning the collective ownership of the earth's resources by all of us, seriously again. Policing and criminal punishment continue to further strip our relationship to the commons, replacing it with private property and heavily circumscribed and policed public property. If we return to an order of knowledge of collective ownership, as the commons previously suggested prior to capitalism, in which we are collectively responsible for managing the natural and social resources that make human life possible, then we will have a different kind of society. This means we would have to transform our thinking about how we care for each other and how we manage conflict and other transgressions.

The idea of the commons brings with it a different kind of moral and ethical order and an abolitionist consciousness demands a different relationship to property as a foundation for radical transformation. In her *New*

York Times essay, Mariame Kaba was at pains to point out that defunding the police was only the first stop on the journey towards abolishing them. My argument is that abolishing the entire carceral system is only a waystation on the long road towards abolishing property and installing new social and economic relations that will allow us to live better together.

The very idea of what constitutes a successful society is currently organized around the private ownership of property, for which an entire apparatus has been developed to perpetuate and protect. At the centre of that apparatus is policing, the legal and court systems, and prisons. If the first police were formed to manage and protect the slave-wealth of white masters by policing the actual body of the Black enslaved person, then the accumulations of modern or even postmodern life now partially transfer those policing practices to managing property and the assumed transgressions against it. What has not changed is that Black and other poor people remain the substantial focus of policing's concerns and thus lie within its dragnet.

Modern policing represents a tremendous subsidy for property owners, one paid for by all citizens through our taxes, including those of us who own no property at all. Once we begin to understand that policing isn't merely about harm reduction, that one of its primary purposes is subsidizing property owners, and that its perpetuation negates another set of possibilities, abolition among them, we become freer to imagine real and different alternatives. Break and enter, vehicle theft, arson, shoplifting, and vandalism are part of a suite of property-related crimes that, when placed alongside street and drug crimes, police use to target poor and Black people. In 2018, the Canadian government reported that:

> After notable increases in property offences in 2015, followed by relative stability in 2016, the rate of property crime has risen more slowly each of the following two years, including an increase of 2% between 2017 and 2018. Property offences with notable rate increases in 2018 were theft over $5,000 (+15%), shoplifting of $5,000 or under (+14%) and fraud (+13%). Their overall impact on the rate of property crime, however, was offset by a 3% decline in mischief and a 1% decline in breaking and entering.[59]

I believe there is a correlation to be made between decreases in poverty and decreases in property crimes. As poverty has decreased in Canada, property crimes have decreased too. Canada's Liberal government reports that one million Canadians were lifted out of poverty by 2015.[60] This claim aligns with the decrease in property crimes over the same period of 2015-2020 when the prime minister made the statement, strongly suggesting that poverty impacts crimes like shoplifting. A sober assessment of what constitutes property crimes leads one to see that an entire carceral system isn't necessary to stem them. Indeed, under different economic and social conditions, where we better care for our least fortunate and most vulnerable, and where we work to right historical wrongs and injustices, these kinds of crimes would largely disappear.

We all worry about violent crimes like robbery, assault and battery, or even murder, even though few of us will ever be subject to them in our lifetimes. It is the threat these crimes represent that is used to justify the ongoing, perverse imbalance of resources allotted to policing and the criminal punishment system. In Canada, the police themselves report that crime has been decreasing since 2009. And it is important to note that even when reports of violent crime have increased for a year here and there, the general long-term trend remains one of steady decline. According to the Government of Canada, "There were over 2.2 million police-reported *Criminal Code* incidents (excluding traffic) reported by police in 2019, about 164,700 more incidents than in 2018. At 5,874 incidents per 100,000 population, the police-re-ported crime rate—which measures the volume of crime—increased 7% in 2019. This rate, however, was still 9% lower than a decade earlier in 2009." The same report further points out that "In 2019, the overall vol-ume and severity of violent crime, as measured by the Violent Crime Severity Index (vcsi), was 89.7, a 7% increase from 2018, but 5% lower than in 2009. The over-all volume and severity of non-violent crime—as measured by the Non-violent csi (nvcsi)—increased 4% in 2019, but was 11% lower than in 2009."[61] If you look at where most of this crime occurred, you would see that it was in communities impacted by poverty. The tragedy of violent crime is that it can be easily identified and inter-cepted if we are willing to invest in the people and communities where it most often occurs.

Though spectacular, violent crime is not what most policing is focused on. The majority of policing is directed towards transgressions against private and public prop-erty. And in vigilantly protecting property, police too often aggressively seek out those who offend, or those they worry might be offending, against it, which has led to deaths like those suffered by Mike Brown, Eric Garner, George Floyd, Andrew Loku, Abdirahman Abdi, Breonna Taylor, Rekia Boyd, Sandra Bland, Korryn Gaines (and, under suspicious circumstances, Regis Korchinski-Paquet in Toronto), and many others too numerous to name. But the problematic relationship between policing and property is even more insidious and damaging than these sensational and well-publicized cases suggests. Not one of the Black people listed above was killed as a result of transgressions against property; but property nevertheless was central to the events that led to their deaths, since each, in varying ways, was viewed as an outsider who should not have been where he or she was, even when they were in their own home. Blaming the victim when police kill them is a part of how police justify use of force. Women are often blamed for sexual assaults committed against them and yet feminists, especially Black and feminists of colour, have led the way on alternatives to policing when dealing with sexual assault and other transgressions.

Sexual assaults present a particularly difficult problem for alternative justice, though this is also one of the main areas in which feminist abolitionists have made important headway. INCITE!, a network of radical feminists organizing against state violence and violence in their communities, has developed a range of resources to avoid police involvement in sexual assault and domestic violence cases. These involve transformative justice approaches that offer a new way of thinking about and dealing with the consequences of sexual assault. Transformative justice and its community accountability processes hold out the promise of a different set of relations when sexual violations occur. Of course, transformative justice is not without its critics. I point to it as a way to demonstrate that policing isn't the only means through which to address this transgression, but I also point to it because communities are already using these practices and thus operating outside of the criminal punishment system as the final arbitrators of how to handle transgressions that cause significant personal harm. Transformative justice's victim-focused community accountability measures do not refuse punishment, but rather allow the parties involved to figure out what punishment might be outside of imprisonment and therefore outside the criminal punishment system. The community at large holds the perpetrator accountable for their transgression and becomes an important part of making the victim as whole as they can possibly be again. If transformative justice can work well with sexual assault, why not with crimes like property transgression, loitering, shoplifting, and so on.

An increase in urban renewal and gentrification-related projects has also meant the expansion of private police, an emblem of prestige in the gated vertical communities otherwise known as condominiums. The privatization of much of our lives has made policing a constant feature of our lives because the scarce resources left for a small number of us and the abandonment of large numbers of people means that conflict is a central element of contemporary social relations. The state of "organized abandonment" in which so many of us live means that we also live with the evidence all around us of others' demise. Policing, broadly defined, allows us to ignore the consequences of such abandonment. The police are called to stop loitering, to keep the unhoused moving, to make sure others do not seek financial help in front of buildings, that they do not rest or sleep. When actual police cannot be there, technological surveillance—and cruder methods like fences, bars, and spikes—stand in to protect property.

We have, since at least the 1980s and the burgeoning of homelessness that began shortly thereafter, witnessed the remaking of public property and space, which has come under threat, with former parks, reserves, and other places being handed over to developers and corporations. But even that space which remains has been rebuilt over the last few decades to socially regulate its use. Shrubbery and thick growth in public parks have been thinned out to guard against misuse; lighting and, in some instances, cameras, have been installed to prevent what some consider antisocial behavior. These changes to public property have targeted the indigent and impacted urban gay male cruising culture, among other cultures. Police now make patrols of these areas a priority in their rounds, again demonstrating that if you look for trouble you can almost certainly find it. These changes have been justified on the grounds of ensuring safety, and reduce the commons even further, making the possibility of us regaining it even that much more difficult.

In the context of neoliberal organized abandonment, homelessness, vagrancy, loitering, lingering, and any practice that marks one as out of place becomes part of the continuum of criminalization. They are the very same exercises of power that were used against post-emancipation Black people to keep them subordinated as cheap wage labourers. These exercises of power have found their most forceful application in the remodelling of public space through public furniture, which, in the last twenty-five years, has been redesigned to prevent the unhoused from sleeping on it. Benches are divided into single seats, protrusions of all kinds added so that sitting too long is uncomfortable. In North America, public washrooms are often locked, while restaurants and cafés are considered private, marked only for paying customers with keys and security door-pad numbers. In many cities, bus shelters have been redesigned so that the unhoused cannot reside in them. At the same time these redesigns are being implemented, a housing crisis in North America has resulted in higher rents and less affordable and publicly funded housing, thus adding to the number of unhoused. The precarity produced by the government's withdrawal of key social services is then made a part of the criminalization continuum. It is these conditions that the abolition of property means to interrupt, and in so doing change the fundamental conditions and priorities of our collective future.

Our idea of property has been reduced so as to become synonymous with real estate, and everything that this entails. We are told that other kinds of property, such as motor cars, boats, jewelry, phones, running shoes, and so on, an immeasurable register of things, need to be protected from those not fortunate enough to own such property. We must be protected from the covetous by the police and the entire carceral system. This is why abolishing property and creating new meanings for and understandings and relationships around the things that make life liveable and enjoyable is central to all abolition-ist claims. Many kinds of criminalization are associated with property, each bringing with it an entire system of punishment. But what if property did not exist in the way we have come to know it? What if it did not exist at all? How else might we come to understand and relate to things? How else would we process and sanction those who transgress against us and our things? It is these kinds of questions that abolition raises, to make more apparent the ways in which we are currently living while freeing us to discover new avenues and answers to create a more caring society. And the first step toward refashioning our relationship to property begins with another encounter with the idea of the commons.

Since what historians have called the enclosure of the commons, where monarchies in Europe appropriated specific lands for their use and benefit, the commons as both an idea and a practical means of organizing life has consistently been reduced to private property. A renewed idea of the commons for our times brings along with it a different idea of care, too, including for the earth itself. Stewardship is an essential aspect of abolition, and in this instance would include collective responsibility for our shared resources as a basis for how we care for each other. Those resources are not only of the earth; they also include the world's technological and accumulated wealth, accrued through more than five hundred years of exploitation of many of us. The realization of this vision of the commons necessitates a profound shift in how we understand life, and abolition is the name we give this wish for transformation. We must recognize that how we presently live together was learned over hundreds of years, which means that it can also be unlearned. We can learn new things, new ways of co-existing. A renewed vision and practice, based on stewardship of the global commons and an ethic of care that begins with attending to the most vulnerable among us first, would open us up to an altogether different, and better way of living together.

This would of course involve a different relationship to property. Our stewardship of the commons would return human beings to our natural place as one species among others. Property would not be owned but would be used to advance the wellbeing of all life forms—human and otherwise. This perspective draws from Indigenous cultures around the world, but it is also significantly influenced by communism insofar as the logic of the communal is what makes it possible. Individualism is a learnt cultural trait and practice; communalism can also be learned and practiced. The change will not happen overnight: what I am outlining here will take time, but I feel strongly that it is the direction that we must move in to ensure our planet's survival.

I will never tire of saying it: property sits at the nexus of our freedom. And not just Black people's freedom. Abolishing property would free all of us and would lead to the establishment of new relationships between people, and between people and animals, the environment, and much else besides. Ruth Wilson Gilmore sees abolition not only as red (as in small-c communism), but also as green: by which she means to signal that abolition's rethinking of how we can live better together includes the development of a green economy as a response to the environmental and ecological disaster we are hurtling towards. Abolition's purpose is to do more than save Black people; it is also to save the species from its self-destructive self. The destruction wrought on this world since millions of Africans, flora, and fauna were transported to the Americas, and the intense, unabated horrors that produced the industrial revolution and our current technological and digital regimes, now require us to fully remake our world if we are to survive. Abolition stands as both the philosophical and practical mode of that urgent remaking.

When I mentioned to a friend that I was writing this pamphlet on the abolition of property he reminded me about the case of Mathieu da Costa. Reputed to be the first Black man to have come to Canada, historians believe da Costa worked as a multilingual translator for Samuel de Champlain. After his service ended, a dispute apparently occurred, and he ended up in a prison in New France. That this first Black person in Canada ended up in prison here seems to me more than a coincidence: his spirit haunts this nation's founding. An outgrowth of the violence of enslavement, the prison in all its permutations continues to subject, subordinate, and dispose of Black life. The Caribbean-American philosopher Sylvia Wynter has argued that the task ahead of us is to reinvent the world as we know it. Abolition is the foundation of that reinvention.

Policing and prisons work to institute and make possible and available the ongoing condemnation of Black life from transatlantic and plantation slavery to the present where we partially represent the wasted populations of post-industrial society. Ever since Africans were forcefully moved to the Americas, our resistance to enslavement has meant that rationalizations, practices, and institutions had to be invented to maintain our subjection. In the post-emancipation period, straight up to our present, those rationalizations, practices, and institutions have mutated into a modern system of debasement, accompanied with new forms of brutality that mark Black life as lesser. By apprehending and upending what we think we know about how society should be ordered, abolition works against the post-emancipation condemnation of Black people and Black life and *unworks* the usual ideas about Black people and our place in the world.

The work of abolition is to make new forms of human life possible. By this we mean that being human is an unfinished project, one that is malleable and revisable. Abolition helps us see this work-in-progress, and to work towards our own betterment. We must open ourselves up to the possibilities of abolition, however much we may initially fear it. Indeed, abolition as an idea has been with us a long time now and it will continue to be with us until it is how we live. The seeds of an abolition to come can now be seen in a number of places and ways of responding, acts of refusal and modes of being.

I would be remiss if I did not point to how these issues play out in social media, where they have had a powerful life. Interventions like "Oscars So White" (#oscarssowhite), for example, benefited from renewed support for Black lives. But these interventions also have their critics, who believe they can slow movement towards a larger abolition politics. Approaches like these merely seek to ensure Black people's equal participation in the world as it presently is, to reap their fair share of the spoils, when the spoils are so obviously part of the problem. So while "Oscars So White" heralds a politics of inclusion and helps bring visibility to Hollywood performers like Lee Daniels, Ava DuVernay, Ryan Coogler, and Jordan Peele, it doesn't help lay the groundwork for the transformation we desperately need.

Referring to Hollywood at this stage in the essay might appear odd; what I mean to show is how some ideas can work to simultaneously broaden our horizons while slowing down real change. In the post-George Floyd world, for instance, demands to defund the police have morphed into calls to hire more non-white police, a strategy we know will not work. Increased inclusion in a corrupt and broken system will do very little to change the system itself. One of the things that strikes me profoundly when I am in a city like Chicago is the large number of Black officers I see. If you walk the city's Golden Mile, an area of expensive boutiques, one will see many police standing outside the shops; many are Black, while the vast majority of shoppers are white people. Modern policing can and does make these kinds of images possible because Black police do not guarantee that Black people will be treated differently by the institution. Recognizing that Black representation does not change institutional practices and behaviour is a pillar of abolitionist thought.

Though the value of social media and so-called hashtag activism is open to debate, I do think it's been essential in popularizing ideas like abolition. Indeed, Mariame Kaba, whose work I have turned to repeatedly here, has used her online presence both to educate and raise funds for abolition and transformative justice efforts as well as other organizations employing these ideas and techniques. These organizations advocate for better low-cost housing, reform of bail conditions, improved and more affordable healthcare, providing books for the incarcerated, infant clothing, and diapers for newborns, among other real life, practical initiatives.

A new ethic of care demands a refusal of the neoliberal individualism that has resulted in increased criminalization and incarceration of the marginalized, much of it race-based, not to mention organized abandonment, mounting poverty, and rising inequality. We must halt further decline of peoples' lives by quickly bridging the gap between what the state refuses to do and what we as ordinary people are capable of doing. A new ethic of care is the suture between the present and a future where full abolition can be realized. These acts of practice, as I would call them, or what Marxists and communists might call agency, are necessary to hold in place the kinds of conditions, ideas, and behaviours that prepare people for abolition.

At this essay's beginning I mentioned the work of Saidiya Hartman, and I return to her now. Hartman is ambivalent about Black agency—since agency is most often associated with the idea of a free person, even an emancipated Black person cannot be understood as being free in the way agency usually implies—and anyone who knows anything about Marxism knows that agency is central to its tenets and particularly to how the working classes can overthrow those who own and control the means of production. In recent years we have seen Black people, influenced by the Movement for Black Lives, attempt not to take over the means of production but

rather to share in them both at the material and ideological level. I have often found myself tweeting "live your
contradictions" as a way to grapple with Black political
demands on the state, its institutions, and its authorizing
mechanisms. For me, "live your contradictions" is one
small way of critiquing movements like #oscarssowhite,
which merely demand inclusion and participation in the
stultifying and indeed death-dealing capitalism of Hollywood. "Oscars So white" is not itself abolitionist but lives
within the context of abolitionist demands for total
transformation.

Conversations about potential Black agency are
always hampered by ideas around racial capital and Black
people's historical and contemporary place as property
inside capitalism. It is the matrix of Black unfreedom,
capitalism, and Black suffering that abolition seeks to
break open, and, in the process, to transform society for
everyone. As a foundational element of the violent invention of blackness, capitalism negatively impacts how
agency, a term deeply wedded to capitalist critique, can
be mobilized to make sense of Black people's desire for
autonomy, bodily and otherwise. But it is my argument
that abolition changes how we conceive of agency. Hartman, in her work with and around agency, often brings
her readers to questions of labour, vagrancy, and idling
as practices that were mobilized by white people with
power to subjugate and subordinate post-slavery Black
people. Hartman's work at the historical level helps us to
see how those same practices have changed but also still
largely underwrite the very conditions now used to support mass criminalization and incarceration. When it
comes to questions of labour, agency meets a certain crit-

ical limit for Black people as a result of our dual role as labouring commodities. But more importantly, questions about agency, or the lack thereof, point to a stalled freedom for Black people, now rearticulated as abolitionist politics and desire, because we are forced to contend with what freedom is or might be, not just for Black people but for everyone.

On the one hand, many Black people, as former and current products of capital and capitalism, continue to believe that we can and should share in the capitalist system, whether as a form of restorative justice or as restitution for suffering a brutal past of bodily theft, psychological and physical terror, and the ongoing devaluation of our lives. Indeed, demand for a justice-based approach that would allow Black people equal participation in the capitalist system, as has been proposed by recent "sub-movements" of the Movement for Black lives like #oscarssowhite, makes sense, but they can never truly transform in the face of other hashtags that continue to mark Black death. Thus, for me #blacklivesmatter and #sayhername are a very different thing than hashtags like #blackgirlmagic and #blackboyjoy and #oscarssowhite. The difference has to do with the desires underlying the invocation. Which desires sit outside capital? Which desires appear to want to be inside of capitalism? Which desires seek to resist and to destroy capitalism? These are crucial questions. What is conditioned by the violence of capital's invention and thus central to my concerns, is Black degradation, disposability, and death. Though #blacklivesmatter and #sayhername are of a different order of desirous politics, and both point for me towards abolition.

We live in a moment where the value of Black human life remains an ongoing question for many who are not Black. Hashtags like #blackboyjoy and #blackgirlmagic draw from the whimsy and fantastic joy of Black life to make a public case for living our lives, and for living them large. But these hashtags also bring with them a certain suspension of critical judgment, coalescing as a collective nod toward Black celebration that quickly moves from the banal, if sometimes surprising, to an easy and unquestioning acceptance of Black people's uncritical participation in capital (here I think of all of the Twitter stories of Black child entrepreneurs, bakers, designers, etc.; child labour celebrated). Indeed, what often gets celebrated under hashtags such as these—access to the crumbs of capital—is anything but magic and joy. Celebrating our participation in capital's margins does not seem to me to be a celebration of Black life. Rather, it marks a kind of perverse self-hatred, one in which capital still devours blackness. But these are the compromises we sometimes need to make. Abolition as a philosophic and actual practice moves beyond such compromises, towards a different kind of settlement.

Hashtags like #blacklivesmatter and #sayhername mark something different for me because they require us to face up to something more profound about our present and past: that we consider the desires, fears, pleasures, joys, wants, and needs, among a range of other things, of Black people everywhere. They force the ongoing question of how Black lives might be valued in the midst of ongoing capitalism and its historically profound anti-Black racist formation, as I have only partially outlined it here. There are those for whom such hashtags might

invoke ideas of capital and restitution, but any real reckoning with Black people's subjection will return to the
scene of the original crime: bodily theft, land theft, genocide and near genocide, primitive accumulation,
capitalism, and so on. And one must then eventually
turn, if one is honest, to abolition as a politics, too. But
these hashtags also turn our attention to genres of the
human: woman, man, boy, girl, trans, persons with dis-
abilities, and on and on, requiring us to think of them
again, and differently. Once more, it boils down to what
kind of economy we want and the necessity for a new
ethic of care. As we rethink and reorganize our lives, it
will become even clearer what must be abolished to make
way for a new, better, and freer kind of existence.

I HAVE WORN dreadlocks since I was about twenty years
of age, or most of my adult life. My locks are both an
identification with Rastafarianism as well as a refusal to
fully give in to Euro-American norms of presentation and
comportment. In short, my locks say something about my
attempt to own myself. As a Black gay man I do not identify with some aspects of Rastafarianism, such as its
patriarchal and homophobic inclinations, but I nonethe-
less still find its fire and brimstone declarations against
white supremacy and capitalism deeply persuasive. What
remains central for me about Rastafarianism is its communal philosophy and anti-capitalist stance. These,
alongside ideas expounded by radical Black feminism,
have been the means through which I have come to
understand that a different, and indeed a better, world is
possible. The women of colour who founded INCITE! have
taught us for over two decades that violence cannot be

the answer to violence; furthermore, they have chal-
lenged us to profoundly rethink what we mean by care
and how we might practice it. Their perspectives have
oriented my thinking and behaviour in profound ways
and influenced my understanding of what abolition can
mean. If we are to have any chance of transforming the
way we live, we need to listen to them. More than that,
we need to join them in their attempt to build the world
we so desperately need.

James Baldwin was no Rastafarian, but he got at the
heart of the matter as much as anyone of his time. "One
day, perhaps," he wrote in 1964, in his essay "Nothing
Personal," "unimaginable generations hence, we will
evolve into the knowledge that human beings are more
important than real estate and will permit this knowledge
to become the ruling principle of our lives. For I do not
for an instant doubt, and I will go to my grave believing,
that we can build Jerusalem, if we will."[62] Abolition, I
strongly believe, is the means of this rebuilding. Ruth
Wilson Gilmore has argued that abolition is not about, as
so many have claimed, taking away anything; rather, it is
concerned with the presence of being—of fully being: the
self needs to be present to others beyond itself. Or, to put
it another way, as Saidiya Hartman has asked, "Is abolition a synonym for love?"[63]

I respond, with absolute certainty, yes.

Notes

1 "Ruth Wilson Gilmore, "Abolition on Stolen Land." *Sawyer Seminar on Sanctuary Spaces: Reworlding Humanism* presented by the UCLA Luskin Institute on Inequality and Democracy, October 9, 2020.

2 David Brion Davis, *Inhuman Bondage* (New York: Oxford University Press, 2006), 331.

3 Davis, *Inhuman Bondage*, 331.

4 Mariame Kaba, "Thinking Through a World Without Police," Transformharm. org, https://transformharm.org/thinking-through-a-world-without-police

5 C L R James, *The Black Jacobins: Toussaint L'Ouverture and the San Domingo Revolution* (New York: Vintage Books, 1989), 95.

6 Davis, *Inhuman Bondage*, 330.

7 Fred Moten, *In The Break: The Aesthetics of the Black Radical Tradition*, (Minneapolis: University of Minnesota Press, 2003).

8 Moten, *In The Break*, 254.

9 Jill Lepore, "The Long Blue Line," *The New Yorker*, July 20, 2020, https://www.newyorker.com/magazine/2020/07/20/the-invention-of-the-police

10 Katherine McKittrick, "Plantation Futures," *Small Axe: A Caribbean Platform for Criticism* 17 (3_42), (November 2013): 1-15.

11 Stephanie E Jones-Rogers, *They Were Her Property: White Women as Slave Owners in the American South* (New Haven: Yale University Press, 2019).

12 Toni Morrison, *Playing in the Dark: Whiteness and the Literary Imagination* (Cambridge: Harvard University Press, 1992), 76.

13 Saidiya Hartman, *Scenes of Subjection: Terror, Slavery and Self-making in Nineteenth Century America* (Oxford: Oxford University Press, 1997), 146.

14 Hartman, *Scenes*, 146.

15 Constance Backhouse, *Colour-coded: A Legal History of Racism in Canada, 1900-1950* (Toronto: University of Toronto Press, 1999), 226.

16 Derek Walcott, *White Egrets* (New York: FSG, 2010), quoted in "These New Plantations By the Sea," Black Atlantic Resource Debate, https://blackatlanticresource.wordpress.com/2010/09/15/these-new-plantations-by-the-sea/

17 Barrington Walker, "Playing the Race Card: Policing Toronto the Good," Torontoist,May5,2015,https://torontoist.com/2015/05/playing-the-race-card-policing-toronto-the-good/

18 Frank Wilderson III, *Red, White and Black: Cinema and the Structure of U.S. Antagonism* (Durham: Duke University Press, 2010), 86.

19 Pierre Bélanger and Kate Yoon, "Canada's Apartheid," *Lapsus Lima*, Novem-

ber 27, 2018, https://www.lapsuslima.com/canadas-apartheid/

20 Brett Popplewell, "A history of missteps," *Toronto Star*, October 30, 2010, https://www.thestar.com/news/investigations/2010/10/30/a_history_of_ missteps.html?rf

21 Mariame Kaba, "Yes, We Mean Literally Abolish the Police," *New York Times*, June 12, 2020, https://www.nytimes.com/2020/06/12/opinion/sunday/ floyd-abolish-defund-police.html

22 As described by the January-February 1993 issue of the *Boston Review*: http:// bostonreview.net/archives/BR18.1/responsibility.html

23 Michelle Alexander, *The New Jim Crow: Mass Incarceration in the Age of Colorblindness* (New York: The New Press, 2010), 28.

24 John Gramlich, "Black imprisonment rate in the U.S. has fallen by a third since 2006," Pew Research Center, May 6, 2020, https://www.pewresearch.org/fact-tank/2020/05/06/share-of-black-white-hispanic-americans-in-prison-2018-vs-2006/

25 Gallup Center on Black Voices, https://news.gallup.com/315575/measuring-black-voices.aspx

26 Kim Tran, "5 Transformative Justice Experts On What We Should Do With 'Sexual Predators' In Our Communities," *Everyday Feminism*, November 16, 2017, https:// everydayfeminism.com/2017/11/me-too-transformative-justice/

27 See, for example, community accountability applied in the case of Malcolm London: https://www.google.com/search?client=safari&rls=en&q=malcom+ london+accoutabilty+proccess&ie=UTF-8&oe=UTF-8

28 Sylvia Wynter, "No Humans Involved: An Open Letter to My Colleagues," *Forum N.H.I. Knowledge for the 21st Century* Vol. 1, No. 1, 1994.

29 Peter Linebaugh and Marcus Rediker, *The Many-Headed Hydra: Sailors, Slaves, Commoners and the Hidden History of the Revolutionary Atlantic.* (Boston: Beacon Press, 2000), 194-195.

30 Davis, *Inhuman Bondage*, 212-213.

31 Davis, *Inhuman Bondage*, 208-209.

32 Davis, *Inhuman Bondage*, 209.

33 Desmond Cole, *The Skin We're In: A Year of Black Resistance and Power* (Toronto: Doubleday Canada, 2019), 60.

34 *A Collective Impact: Interim report on the inquiry into racial profiling and racial discrimination of Black persons by the Toronto Police Service.* Toronto: Ontario Human Rights Commission, 2018, http://www.ohrc.on.ca/en/public-interest-inquiry-racial-profiling-and-discrimination-toronto-police-service/ collective-impact-interim-report-inquiry-racial-profiling-and-racial-discrimination-black

35 Judith Sunderland, "They Talk to Us Like We're Dogs: Abuse Police Stops in France," Human Rights Watch, June 18, 2020, https://www.hrw.org/ report/2020/06/18/they-talk-us-were-dogs/abusive-police-stops-france

36 Reuters, "Riot police fire teargas on anti-racism protestors in Paris," *The Guardian*, June 13, 2020, https://www.theguardian.com/world/2020/ jun/13/riot-police-fire-teargas-on-anti-racism-protesters-in-paris

37 Martin Luther King Jr, "The Other America," Stanford University, April 14, 1967, https://www.crmvet.org/docs/otheram.htm

38 "Angela Davis on Abolition, Calls to Defund the Police," *Democracy Now*, July 3, 2020, https://www.democracynow.org/2020/7/3/angela_davis_on_ abolition_calls_to

39 Kaba, "Yes, We Mean Literally Abolish the Police"

40 Amelia Cheatham and Lindsay Maizland, "How Police Compare in Different Democracies," Council on Foreign Relations, updated November 12, 2020,

https://www.cfr.org/backgrounder/how-police-compare-different-democracie

41 *Expenditure Analysis of Criminal Justice in Canada.* Ottawa: Office of the Parliamentary Budget Officer, 2013, http://www.pbo-dpb.gc.ca/web/default/files/files/files/Crime_Cost_EN.pdf. In 2017 the Trudeau government split this department into two departments—Crown-Indigenous Relations and Northern Affairs and Indigenous Services. There was also an earlier change from Aboriginal to Indigenous as well.

42 Cheatham and Maizland, "How Police Compare"

43 Jacques Marcoux and Katie Nicholson, "Deadly Force: Fatal encounters with police in Canada: 2000-2017," CBC News, https://newsinteractives.cbc.ca/longform-custom/deadly-force

44 Kelly Geraldine Malone, Meredith Omstead and Liam Casey, "Police shootings in 2020: The effect on officers and those they are sworn to protect," CBC News, December 21, 2020, https://www.cbc.ca/news/canada/manitoba/police-shootings-2020-yer-review-1.5849788

45 Angela Davis, *Are Prisons Obsolete?* (New York: Seven Stories Press, 2003), 10.

46 Davis, *Are Prisons Obsolete?*, 15.

47 Ruth Wilson Gilmore, *Golden Gulag: Prisons, Surplus, Crisis, and Opposition in Globalizing California*, (Berkeley: University of California Press, 2007), 7.

48 *Statistics: Staff Ethnicity/Race*, Federal Bureau of Prisons, https://www.bop.gov/about/statistics/statistics_staff_ethnicity_race.jsp

49 Rachel Gandy, "In prisons, Blacks and Latinos do the time while whites get the jobs," Prison Policy Initiative, July 10, 2015, https://www.prisonpolicy.org/blog/2015/07/10/staff_disparities/

50 Gilmore, *Golden Gulag*, 26.

51 "Data on Canada's prison system," The John Howard Society of Canada, January 25, 2020, https://johnhoward.ca/blog/data-on-canadas-prison-system

52 "Data on Canada's prison system"

53 Jamil Malakieh, Adult and youth correctional statistics in Canada, 2017/2018, Statistics Canada, May 9, 2019, https://www150.statcan.gc.ca/n1/pub/85-002-x/2019001/article/00010-eng.htm

54 "Data on Canada's prison system"

55 *A Case Study of Diversity in Corrections: The Black Inmate Experience in Federal Penitentiaries Final Report*, Office of the Correctional Investigator, https://www.oci-bec.gc.ca/cnt/rpt/oth-aut/oth-aut20131126-eng.aspx

56 Egbert Gaye, "Too Many Blacks in Canadian Prisons," *Montreal Community Contact*, January 27, 2020, http://montrealcommunitycontact.com/too-many-blacks-in-canadian-prisons/

57 Gilmore, *Golden Gulag*, 107.

58 "Data on Canada's prison system"

59 Greg Moreau, *Police-reported crime statistics in Canada, 2018*, Statistics Canada, July 22, 2019, https://www150.statcan.gc.ca/n1/pub/85-002-x/2019001/article/00013-eng.htm

60 "More than 1 million Canadians lifted out of poverty," Office of the Prime Minister, March 5, 2020, https://pm.gc.ca/en/news/news-releases/2020/03/05/more-1-million-canadians-lifted-out-poverty

61 Malakieh, Adult and youth correctional statistics in Canada

62 James Baldwin, "Nothing Personal." *Baldwin: Collected Essays* (New York: Library of America, 1998), 704.

63 Saidiya Hartman, "The End of White Supremacy, An American Romance," BOMB, June 5, 2020, https://bombmagazine.org/articles/the-end-of-white-supremacy-an-american-romance/

Acknowledgements

WHEN DAN WELLS approached me and asked if I would extend a comment I made in a CBC Radio interview about policing and the abolition of property, I said yes right away. When Dan explained he was reviving the pamphlet as a genre or form in a series of short books, he could not have known at that moment what pleasure he was sending my way. You see, I have always wanted to write a pamphlet in the tradition of those I had read about as a child, concerning the great Black and white abolitionists of slavery and how they got the word out about their cause. To pen a pamphlet that continues the debate on abolition and the historic unfinished project of abolition for Black people gave me immense political joy. I want to thank my friend Cecil Foster for the initial introduction to Dan.

This pamphlet on the abolition of property argues that it is not just the police we want to abolish but the entire system that requires police in the first instance. And furthermore, I suggest that abolishing property is the unfinished goal of my Black ancestors who initiated the project of abolition that other generations will bring to its logical end—a reordering of planetary life. One of the decisions I made in writing this work was to draw largely on internet resources as opposed to academic sources so that readers with access to the internet could access the sources I used to make my argument. One of the important things to note about an abolition consciousness and sensibility is that it remains open to sharing, open to what it does not yet know and open to ongoing revision. Abolition is not an arrival: it is an ongoing practice of rethinking through a logic of care that exists beyond the self.

I thank Dan Wells enormously for sticking with me and this pamphlet. He has been a tremendous reader, questioner, editor, and publisher. I also thank the many Black women abolitionists who I have learned from, some of them quoted in these pages, others not, who have consistently demonstrated to me that Black radical politics does not only assess our present, but is the blueprint for a future we all need. In particular, Black radical feminists are more than a vanguard. They are the intellectual guides for how to live better together; we neglect their political organizing, their intellectual insights, and their models for living differently together right now at our own peril.

I thank my partner Abdi Osman, who had to eat a lot of ordered out meals in the last few weeks as I worked on this pamphlet. And I thank the staff at Biblioasis, whose diligence is unmatched.

This work is for the generations to come who will bring down Babylon.

RINALDO WALCOTT is a Professor in the Women and Gender Studies Institute at the University of Toronto. His research is in the area of Black Diaspora Cultural Studies, gender and sexuality.

MIX
Paper
FSC® C100212

Printed by Imprimerie Gauvin
Gatineau, Québec